KNITTING
WRAPS
in the round

T0267315

KNITTING WRAPS

in the round

21 inspired SHAWLS, SCARVES, AND STOLES

Andrea Brauneis

Stackpole
Books

Essex, Connecticut
Blue Ridge Summit, Pennsylvania

STACKPOLE BOOKS

An imprint of Globe Pequot, the trade division of The Rowman & Littlefield Publishing Group, Inc.
4501 Forbes Blvd., Ste. 200
Lanham, MD 20706
www.rowman.com

Distributed by NATIONAL BOOK NETWORK
800-462-6420

EIN BUCH DER
EDITION MICHAEL FISCHER

Copyright © 2020 Edition Michael Fischer, Gmbh, www.emf-verlag.de
This edition of *Tücher in Runden stricken* first published in Germany by Edition Michael Fischer Gmbh in
2020 is published by arrangement with Silke Bruenink Agency, Munich, Germany.

Cover design and typesetting: Bernadett Linseisen and Sally Rinehart
Product management: Anja Sommerfeld
Editing: Ute Wielandt
Images: © Corinna Brix, Munich
Author photograph: © Andrea Brauneis
Translation: Katharina Sokiran

All rights reserved. No part of this book may be reproduced in any form or by any electronic or mechanical
means, including information storage and retrieval systems, without written permission from the publisher,
except by a reviewer who may quote passages in a review.

The contents of this book are for personal use only. Patterns herein may be reproduced in limited quanti-
ties for such use. Any large-scale commercial reproduction is prohibited without the written consent of the
publisher.

We have made every effort to ensure the accuracy and completeness of these instructions. We cannot,
however, be responsible for human error, typographical mistakes, or variations in individual work.

British Library Cataloguing in Publication Information available

Library of Congress Cataloging-in-Publication Data available

ISBN 978-0-8117-7045-3 (paper : alk. paper)
ISBN 978-0-8117-7046-0 (electronic)

First Edition

♡ **CONTENTS**

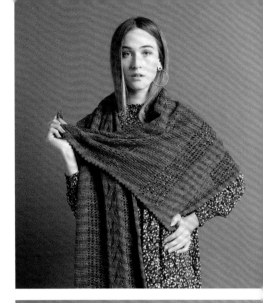

KNITTING IS MY *Passion.*

I live this passion every day, always looking out for innovation, inspiration, and ideas, including those from international sources. This is how some time ago I happened to stumble upon a knitting technique from Norway called "steeking." Here, knitted pieces, mostly cardigans and shawls, are worked in the round, often in stranded colorwork patterns, with extra stitches added in places where an opening is needed. These additional stitches, called the "steek," are later cut through in the middle, after which the beauty of the knitted piece can unfold entirely.

Once I had started, I very quickly saw the many advantages this knitting technique has to offer—there are no annoying purl rows, stitch patterns that would be complicated to work in back-and-forth rows can be effortlessly accomplished, stitch definition is much improved, tedious weaving in of ends can be almost completely eliminated, and the knitting process itself is pleasant and relaxing.

Whenever possible, I knit a piece steeked. This year, we spent our family vacation in Norway, where I was able to draw more inspiration for this fabulous way of knitting and further broaden my knowledge of the technique.

With this book, I want to open the door into the world of steeking just ever so slightly for you. Slip through with me, and discover how relaxing and exciting at the same time knitting in the round and steeking can be.

In this book, you will find wraps worked in the round, from very simple knit-and-purl patterns through stranded colorwork to rather challenging lace patterns, from airy summer shawls to cozily warm wraps for the colder season.

Now, I wish you a pleasant time in picking out your wrap and many rounds of enjoyable, relaxing knitting after that.

Wear your creation with pride, and let all your friends know how enjoyable it is to knit steeked wraps!

I'm looking forward to seeing your posts with photographs of your projects and your interpretations of my designs.

Happy Knitting!

Yours truly,

Andrea Brauneis

Materials and Knitting Basics

BEFORE YOU BEGIN

CHOOSING THE YARN

The most important factor for steeking is choosing the right material. I highly recommend that you use a yarn with a fiber content of 100% wool or at least a very high percentage of wool. In Norway, where this technique originates, traditional Norwegian ethnic patterns are almost exclusively worked in Shetlandic or Icelandic wool. With this grippy yarn, it is even possible to cut the steek without securing it first since this yarn does not unravel easily and is prone to felting quickly, owing to its numerous short staples. In our more moderate climate, however, we are more inclined to use yarns with mixed fiber content, plant-based yarns or those of synthetic origin, so it is essential to secure steek stitches with seams. As a matter of fact, a stitch cut through will always only unravel vertically, never horizontally. Nevertheless, I would very much like to recommend that you pick a yarn that meets the requirements for steeking. The knitting and fiber world has indeed dramatically changed in the last years—the trend is moving again toward real wool, away from synthetic fiber. Yarns that have been ecologically sourced and are suitable for those with allergies have hit the market, so there is a wide range for you to choose from. For the wraps in this book, I have chosen yarns consisting almost exclusively of wool and that come in a broad color range. Another important aspect for me is that the finished shawl or wrap should not feel scratchy when worn next to the skin around your neck and shoulders. But, of course, there are no limits to your creativity and own imagination, and every piece can be worked in the material of your personal preference.

BLOCKING THE SHAWL

When you have finished knitting up your wrap, it will need to be washed and blocked, since it can bloom into its true beauty only after this procedure. Stitch definition will improve, stranded colorwork patterns will end up in correct alignment, and delicate lace patterns will open up only after having been washed, and the steek seam, too, will be flattened and look neater.

For this, wash your shawl according to the manufacturer's directions found on the yarn wrapper, let it soak for a short time (in most cases in lukewarm water), lightly press to remove excess water, and roll it up in a towel. During the latter, you can still gently press out more water. Afterward, spread out your wrap on an even horizontal surface, and block it to the indicated measurements. Don't be greedy with blocking pins here—the more of them you use to open up the stitch patterns, the better the result will look. In addition to actual blocking mats, foam puzzle floor mats are well suited for this purpose. Since these are made of foam rubber, they are great for use with T-pins or blocking wires. Do let the shawl completely dry before unpinning it.

GAUGE SWATCH

While a specific gauge is listed for every pattern, this should only be used as a guideline. Take the time to prepare a gauge swatch to find out whether the needle size listed in the instructions will suit your knitting style or whether you have to use a different size to achieve matching gauge. If substituting yarns, you can also find out beforehand whether the yarn is a good match for the pattern and see whether the result is to your liking. Small gauge differences are not a big deal for a shawl or wrap—yours would just be minimally smaller or larger than the original. You can also use your gauge swatch as a washing and blocking sample by washing it according to the manufacturer's directions and then blocking it to see how the material changes, whether the color bleeds, or whether the yarn itself will "bloom," or turn softer or smoother.

THE RIGHT TOOLS

Although you will probably already be well equipped with everything you need for knitting, there are a few useful tools that will make work easier for you, and you might consider them useful additions to your work basket. For steeked wraps, you will always need either a DPN set in a matching size or short circular needles for the first few rows of the piece. In subsequent rows, there will be more stitches on account of the increases, and soon you will need circular needles in different lengths, starting with a cord length of 16 in (40 cm) up to 60 in (150 cm). A big advantage for this type of project will be an interchangeable needle set, which allows for attaching different needle tips to cables of the required length. You will also need basic notions, such as stitch markers, to be used when necessary, a cable needle or other auxiliary needle, a measuring tape, and a tapestry needle. For those projects using stranded colorwork, a yarn guide is very useful: it prevents the working yarns from tangling and feeds them at an even tension. One tool you should not be without is a high-quality pair of sharp scissors with pointy blades that can cut the steek in the exact spot needed. Having them will make life much easier when it comes to further finishing your steek.

ADDITIONAL TOOLS

1. Flexible-cable circular needles

2. Stitch markers

3. Yarn guide or knitting thimble for stranded colorwork with up to 4 strands

4. Yarn guide or knitting thimble for stranded colorwork with up to 2 strands

5. Crochet hooks in different sizes

6. Tapestry needles or sewing needles

7. Embroidery scissors

8. Knitting needle gauge

9. Fabric scissors

10. Measuring tape

STEEKING

Steeking originates in picturesque Norway, where the most beautiful stranded color-work patterns are designed and knit using traditional knitting techniques tried and tested over time. Cardigans, for instance, are knit in the round there, adding a few additional stitches to the round in spots where an opening is needed. Later, these stitches are cut through with scissors. Why go to the trouble? you may ask yourself now. Perhaps the thought of cutting with sharp scissors through the knitted piece you've just worked so hard to create will even trigger beads of sweat on your forehead. Do not fear; I can tell you from experience that steeking is a very enjoyable activity that will give you strength, since with every step, you will become more courageous, and courage is good for you!

You will also notice that your knitted piece will, amazingly, not disintegrate into its components but unfold in its complete beauty.

Steeking has numerous advantages. It is more efficient and much easier to knit in the round since the cumbersome wrong-side rows can be skipped. For stranded colorwork patterns, for instance, this is a wonderful thing: since you only knit on the outside of the piece, the color sequence is always visible and never obstructed by floats. Complicated lace or Japanese stitch patterns can be easily worked this way too. Patterns that you would not have dared to attempt in back-and-forth rows can be mastered easily. Stitch definition is much more homogenous, and even the now-fashionable two-color brioche will be a breeze. The process is incredibly relaxing, and with every new round worked, you will look forward with anticipation to the time coming to cut through the steek.

THE STEEK

In the photo below, you can see a swatch in stranded colorwork, connected by a steek. This is the striped column of stitches between the selvedge stitches. In stranded colorwork, it is important to always work the steek stitches in alternating colors to avoid long floats, which would be in the way when cutting later and prevent a neat finishing.

SECURING THE STEEK

To make sure that indeed not a single stitch will unravel, and especially to secure yarns not composed of 100% wool fiber, it is essential to border the steek with two securing seams. For shawls and wraps, a machine- or hand-sewn steek seam works best. This produces a neat-looking seam.

HAND-SEWN STEEK

Place a straight or back stitch directly into the steek stitch adjacent to the selvedge stitch. Doubly secure the first and last stitches by looping around the base of the knit stitch twice. Now, to sew a back stitch, insert the needle into the next stitch from top to bottom in the center of the knit stitch between the strands that form the stitch, and lead the needle up again through the next stitch. Pull the sewing thread through. Now, insert the needle in the next-to-last exit point, and lead the needle through the second stitch from the bottom up. Pull the sewing thread through again. Repeat these steps for the length of your steek. Make sure to grasp the bases of all knit stitches.

MACHINE-SEWN STEEK

If using a regular sewing machine, before cutting, place a zigzag seam directly in the first steek stitch next to the selvedge stitch. The neatest and most reliable method, though, is to secure the edges of the cut with a serger. This will ensure that no stitch will unravel. If you own a serger, I strongly recommend employing it for this purpose. However, with a serger, this can only be done after the steek has already been cut (see next paragraph).

CUTTING THE STEEK

Now, using pointy, sharp scissors, cut through the middle one of the steek stitches. For a steek width of, for instance, 9 stitches, leave 4 stitches each to both sides, and cut through the middle of the 5th stitch. Afterward, neatly finish the steek according to the instructions.

KNITTING STITCHES TOGETHER

1. Insert the right needle from left to right first into the stitch after the next one and then into the next stitch on the left needle.

2. Pull the working yarn through as if to knit.

3. Let both stitches slip off the left needle. Three or more stitches can be knitted together the same way too.

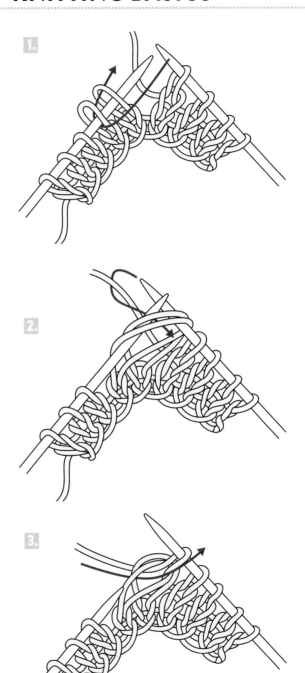

PURLING TWO OR MORE STITCHES TOGETHER

Insert the right needle from right to left into the next two stitches, and pull the working yarn through as if to purl. Let the stitches slip off the left needle.

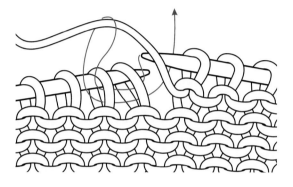

KNITTING A STITCH THROUGH THE FRONT AND BACK TO INCREASE

1. Insert the right needle into the next stitch as if to knit . . .

2. . . . and pull the working yarn through.

3. Without letting the stitch slip off the left needle . . .

4. . . . knit the same stitch once more through the back loop (through the leg of the stitch farther away from you).

5. Now, let the stitch slip off the left needle.

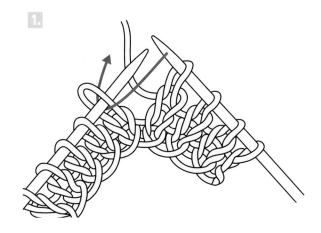

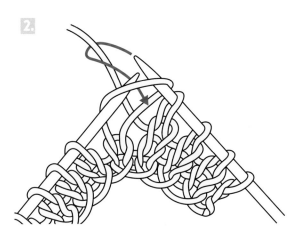

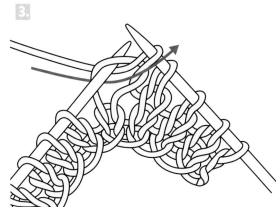

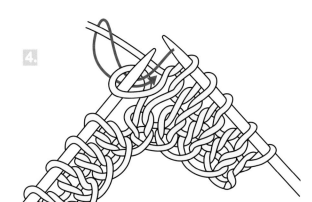

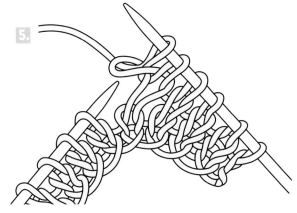

KNITTED CAST-ON

1. Knit the stitch originally cast on (slipknot) or the stitch of the current row, but still leave it on the left needle.

2. Twist the new loop clockwise . . .

3. . . . and place it on the left needle.

For each stitch to be cast on this way, repeat all steps, starting at step 1.

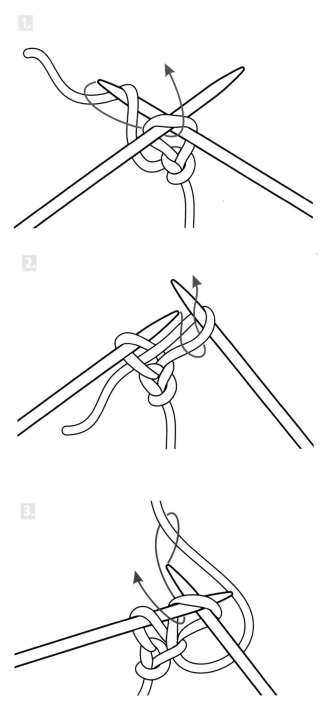

PICKING UP STITCHES FROM THE SELVEDGE

When picking up stitches from the side edge of a knitted piece, please note: stitches in knitted fabric will in most cases be more wide than tall.

If you were to pick up one stitch from every row in the knitting, the row from the picked-up stitches would have too many stitches. It would turn out wavy. To knit on a sideways band or facing, it is recommended that you prepare for it in advance during knitting by working an all-knit or all-purl selvedge without slipping any selvedge stitches. This produces one solid stitch for every row, from which it is easier to pick up and knit.

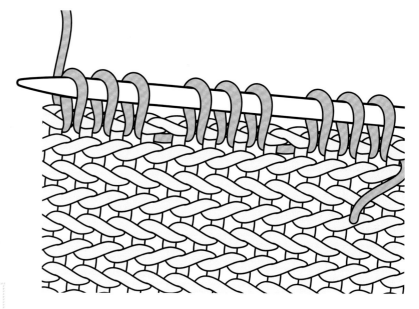

Tip

If you intend to work the band in a contrasting color, first pick up the stitches in the old color and then change to the new color and work the next row in the contrasting color. This creates a much neater and less noticeable transition.

Please note

The stitch-to-row ratio will be about 1:2 for pieces worked in garter stitch and about 3:4 for those in stockinette. The exact ratio can be derived from your gauge.

BINDING OFF IN APPLIED I-CORD

1. At the end of the last row, cast on two new stitches using the backward loop cast-on method.

2. Turn your work. Knit the two newly cast-on stitches.

3. Slip the third and fourth stitch individually to the right needle, return them to the left needle, and knit them together through the back loop. Return all stitches to the left needle. Now, work these stitches again as follows:

4. Knit the first and the second stitch, ssk (see Abbreviations) the third and fourth stitch. Repeat these steps.

5. This is how the finished i-cord edge will look.

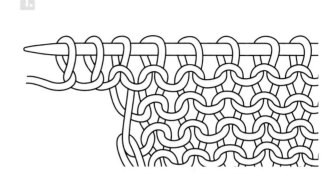

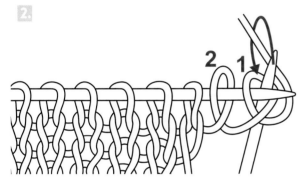

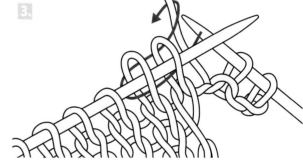

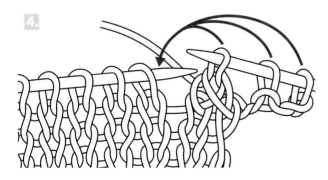

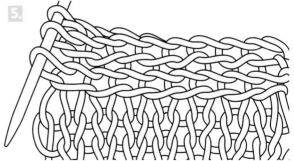

REGULAR BIND-OFF WITH PASSED-OVER STITCHES

1. Knit the first two stitches; then insert the left needle from left to right into the first one of the two worked stitches.

2. Pass this stitch over the one located to the left of it, and off the left needle. One stitch has been bound off. Knit the next stitch, and again pass the stitch to the right of it over it.

3. Repeat these steps to the end of the row. Now, break the working yarn, leaving an end of about 4 in (10 cm) to be woven in later, and thread this tail through the last loop.

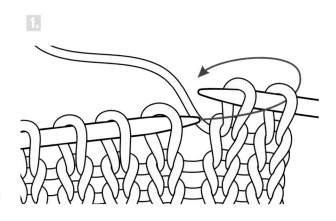

Please note

Binding off in purl or in pattern is worked using the same principle. Stitches are worked as they appear: knit stitches in knit and purl stitches in purl.

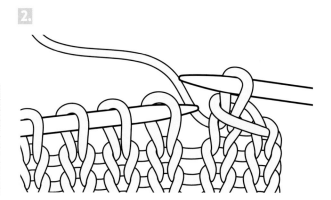

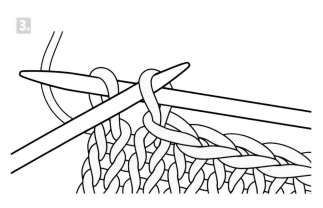

ELASTIC BIND-OFF WITH PASSED-OVER STITCHES

1. Work as for regular bind-off with passed-over stitches, but do not drop the passed-over stitch from the left needle. Bypassing this stitch, work the following stitch. You will have two stitches on your right needle and the original passed-over stitch on the left needle.

2. Use your left needle to pass the far-right stitch from the right needle over the left stitch on the right needle, and let this stitch and the passed-over stitch still on the left needle slip off the left needle together.

3. Repeat steps 1 and 2 to the end of the row. This trick will help you to create a stretchy bind-off edge.

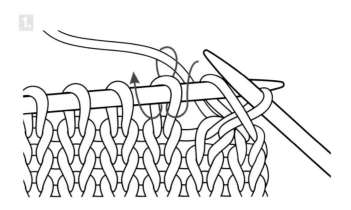

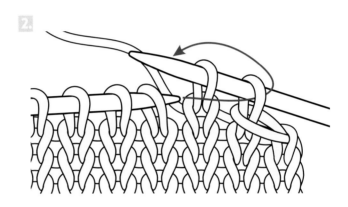

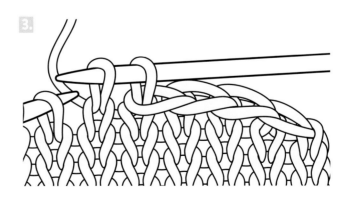

ABBREVIATIONS

bar	=	bar between stitches
BO	=	bind off
brk	=	brioche knit
brp	=	brioche purl
CO	=	cast on
ctr st(s)	=	center stitch(es)
DPN(s)	=	double-pointed needle(s)
k	=	knit
M1-k	=	make 1 knitwise from the bar between stitches, twisted
M1-p	=	make 1 purlwise from the bar between stitches, twisted
N	=	nupp(s)
ndl	=	needle(s)
patt	=	pattern
p	=	purl
p/u	=	pick up
rep	=	repeat
rnd(s)	=	round(s)
RS	=	right side
selv st	=	selvedge stitch
skp	=	slip, knit, pass
sl	=	slip
ssk	=	slip, slip, knit
sssk	=	slip, slip, slip, knit
st(s)	=	stitch(es)
stk-st(s)	=	steek stitch(es)
tbl	=	through the back loop
tog	=	together
WS	=	wrong side
wyib	=	with yarn in back of work
wyif	=	with yarn in front of work
yo	=	yarn over

DIFFICULTY LEVELS

easy

requires some practice

for experienced knitters

SYMBOL KEY

▣ knit 1 stitch

⊡ purl 1 stitch

◙ knit 1 stitch through the back loop

◎ 1 yarn over

■ 1 selvedge stitch

◙ 1 slipped stitch = slip 1 stitch as if to purl, with yarn in front of work

◀ slip 1 stitch as if to knit, with yarn in back of work

◆ increase 1 stitch from the bar between stitches

◢ knit 2 stitches together right-leaning

◣ knit 2 stitches together left-leaning with passing over (skp): slip 1 stitch, knit 1 stitch, and then pass the slipped stitch over the knitted one

◢ knit 2 stitches together left-leaning (ssk)

◤ knit 3 stitches together left-leaning (sssk)

◤ knit 3 stitches together left-leaning with passing over (sk2p)

◣ knit the yarn over through the back loop (twisted)

☐ no stitch, for better overview only

3-stitch mini cable: insert the right needle into the 3rd stitch and pass it to the right, over the 2nd and 1st stitch and off the needle; knit the 1st stitch, make a yarn over, knit the 2nd stitch

hold 4 stitches on cable needle behind work, purl 1, knit 2, purl 1; then work the stitches from the cable needle as: purl 1, knit 2, purl 1

hold 4 stitches on cable needle in front of work, purl 1, knit 2, purl 1; then work the stitches from the cable needle as: purl 1, knit 2, purl 1

hold 6 stitches on cable needle behind work, knit 1-tbl, purl 1, knit 1-tbl, purl 1, knit 1-tbl, purl 1, knit 1-tbl; then work the stitches from the cable needle as: purl 1, knit 1-tbl, purl 1, knit 1-tbl, purl 1, knit 1-tbl

Projects

Fleur

FAIR-ISLE SHAWL
WITH EYELET BANDS

Basics

FINISHED SIZE
90.6 x 29.5 in (230 x 75 cm)

TOOLS AND MATERIALS
▸ Lang Yarns Baby Alpaca (100% alpaca; 185 yd/169 m, 1.75 oz/50 g per skein); 5 skeins #0050 Mustard Yellow and 3 skeins #0094 White
▸ Circular knitting needles, size US 4 (3.5 mm) in different lengths
▸ DPN set, size US 4 (3.5 mm)
▸ Yarn guide for stranded colorwork
▸ Stitch markers as needed
▸ Scissors
▸ Tapestry needle for weaving in ends

STITCH PATTERNS
Stockinette stitch: In rows: knit on RS, purl on WS; in rounds: knit all sts in all rounds.
Stranded colorwork pattern: Work from chart. Repeat patt sts as indicated. All rounds are shown in the chart, and the chart is to be read from right to left.
Steek stitches: Worked as knit sts and not counted in the stitch count.
Selvedge stitches: In rows: knit on RS, purl on WS; in rounds: knit all selv sts in all rounds.

GAUGE
In stockinette stitch on US 4 (3.5 mm) needles:
26 sts and 34 rows = 4 x 4 in (10 x 10 cm)

Instructions

CO 4 sts in Mustard Yellow.
Row 1: Selv st, yo, k2, yo, selv st. (6 sts)
Row 2: Selv st, yo, p-tbl of yo, p2, p-tbl of yo, yo, selv st. (8 sts)
Row 3: Selv st, yo, k-tbl of yo, k4, k-tbl of yo, yo, selv st. (10 sts)
Row 4: Selv st, yo, p-tbl of yo, p6, p-tbl of yo, yo, selv st. (12 sts)
Row 5: Selv st, yo, k-tbl of yo, k8, k-tbl of yo, yo, selv st. (14 sts)
After this row, CO 9 additional sts for the steek, distribute sts onto a DPN set, and join into the round.
Rnd 6: Selv st, yo, k-tbl of yo, k10, k-tbl of yo, selv st, stk-sts. (16 sts)
Rnds 7–20: As Rnd 6; the number of knit sts in the middle increases by 2 with every rnd worked. (44 sts)
Rnd 21: In White, selv st, yo, k-tbl of yo, k40, k-tbl of yo, yo, selv st, stk-sts. (46 sts)
Rnd 22: Selv st, yo, p-tbl of yo, p42, p-tbl of yo, yo, selv st, stk-sts. (48 sts)
Rnd 23: Selv st, yo, k-tbl of yo, * skp, yo *, rep from * to * 21 times more, k-tbl of yo, yo, selv st, stk-sts. (50 sts)
Rnd 24: Selv st, yo, p-tbl of yo, p46, p-tbl of yo, yo, selv st, stk-sts. (52 sts)

Rnds 25–48: In Mustard Yellow, work as Rnd 6. (100 sts)
Rnds 49–52: In White, work as Rnds 21–24. (108 sts)
Rnds 53–74: In Mustard Yellow, work as Rnd 6. (152 sts)
Rnds 75–78: In White, work as Rnds 21–24. (160 sts)
Rnds 79–100: In Mustard Yellow, work as Rnd 6. (204 sts)
Rnds 101–104: In White, work as Rnds 21–24. (212 sts)
Rnd 105: Stranded colorwork strip #1: selv st, yo, k-tbl of yo, work sts 11–19 of Rnd 1 of the colorwork chart once, work the whole patt rep 10 times, work sts 1–9 of the colorwork chart once, k-tbl of yo, yo, selv st, stk-sts. (214 sts)
Rnds 106–119: Work according to chart, and as Rnd 105. At the beginning and the end of every rnd, always work 1 st more of the patt rep. In Rnd 106, this means to work at the beginning of the rnd, sts 10–19, and at the end, sts 1–10; in Rnd 107, at the beginning, sts 9–19 of the patt rep, and at the end, sts 1–11, etc. (242 sts)
Rnds 120–123: In White, work as Rnds 21–24. (250 sts)

Rnds 124–145: In Mustard Yellow, work as Rnd 6. (294 sts)

Rnds 146–149: In White, work as Rnds 21–24. (302 sts)

Rnds 150–171: In Mustard Yellow, work as Rnd 6. (346 sts)

Rnds 172–175: In White, work as Rnds 21–24. (354 sts)

Rnd 176: Stranded colorwork strip #2: selv st, yo, k-tbl of yo, work sts 16–19 of Rnd 1 of the colorwork chart once, the patt rep 18 times, sts 1–4 of the patt rep once, k-tbl of yo, yo, selv st, stk-sts. (356 sts)

Rnds 177–190: Work according to chart, and as Rnd 176, incorporating sts increased at the beginning and the end of the rnd into the patt. (384 sts)

Rnds 191–194: In White, work as Rnds 21–24. (392 sts)

Rnds 195–216: In Mustard Yellow, work as Rnd 6. (436 sts)

Rnds 217–220: In White, work as Rnds 21–24. (444 sts)

Rnd 221: Stranded colorwork strip #3: selv st, yo, k-tbl of yo, work sts 18–19 of Rnd 1 of the colorwork chart once, the patt rep 23 times, and st 1 of the patt rep once, k-tbl of yo, yo, selv st, stk-sts. (446 sts)

Rnds 222–235: Work according to chart, and as Rnd 221, incorporating sts increased at the beginning and the end of the rnd into the patt. (474 sts)

Rnds 236–239: In White, work as Rnds 21–24. (482 sts)

In the last rnd, BO the steek sts the regular way, and BO the 482 other sts with applied i-cord edging (see p. 23).

FINISHING

Now, secure the steek as described in Basics (pp. 16–17); then cut it. Fold over the stk-sts to the WS twice, pin, and sew on. Wash the wrap according to the manufacturer's recommendations on the ball band of the yarn, pin it to block, and let it dry.

COLORWORK CHART

Chart columns (right to left): 19 18 17 16 15 14 13 12 11 10 9 8 7 6 5 4 3 2 1
Chart rows (bottom to top): 1 2 3 4 5 6 7 8 9 10 11 12 13 14 15

Maia
TWO-COLOR BRIOCHE SHAWL

Basics

FINISHED SIZE
67 x 27.6 in (170 x 70 cm)

TOOLS AND MATERIALS
▶ Ito Yarn Shimo (80% wool, 20% silk; 291 yd/266 m, 1.75 oz/50 g per skein); 2 skeins #843 Watermint and 2 skeins #846 Charcoal
▶ Circular knitting needles, US size 4 (3.5 mm) in different lengths
▶ DPN set, US size 4 (3.5 mm)
▶ Stitch markers as needed
▶ Scissors
▶ Tapestry needle for weaving in ends

STITCH PATTERNS
Garter stitch: In rows: knit on RS and on WS; in rounds, alternate—Rnd 1: knit; Rnd 2: purl.

Brioche knit (brk): Rnd 1: k1, Rnd 2: insert the right needle from front to back into the stitch 1 rnd below the st to be worked, pull the working yarn through this st, and lift it onto the right needle. This dissolves the st above and places it like a yarn over, onto the needle.

Brioche purl (brp): Rnd 1: p1, Rnd 2: insert the right needle from back to front into the stitch 1 rnd below the st to be worked, pull the working yarn through this st, and lift it onto the right needle. This dissolves the st above and places it like a yarn over, onto the needle.

Steek stitches: Worked as knit sts and not counted in the stitch count.

Selvedge stitches: Knit on RS, purl on WS (in rounds of garter stitch, i.e., purl in odd-numbered rounds and knit in even-numbered rounds).

GAUGE
In stockinette stitch on US 4 (3.5 mm) needles:
23 sts and 34 rows = 4 x 4 in (10 x 10 cm)

Instructions

CO 5 sts in Watermint.
Row 1: Selv st, k1, M1-k, k1, M1-k, k1, selv st. (7 sts)
Row 2: Selv st, k1, M1-k, k3, M1-k, k1, selv st. (9 sts)
Row 3: Selv st, k1, M1-k, k5, M1-k, k1, selv st. (11 sts)
Row 4: Selv st, k2, M1-k, k2, M1-k, p1 (ctr-st), M1-k, k2, M1-k, k2, selv st. (15 sts)
Row 5: Selv st, k6, k1 (ctr-st), k6, selv st.
Row 6: Selv st, k2, M1-k, k4, M1-k, p1 (ctr-st), M1-k, k4, M1-k, k2, selv st. (19 sts)
After this row, CO 9 additional sts for the steek, distribute sts onto a DPN set, and join into the round.
Rnd 7: P9, k1 (ctr-st), p9, k9 (stk-sts).
Rnd 8: K3, M1-k, k6, M1-k, k1 (ctr-st), M1-k, k6, M1-k, k3, k9 (stk-sts). (23 sts)

Rnd 9: P11, k1 (ctr-st), p11, k9 (stk-sts).
Rnds 10–29: Rep Rnds 8–9 another 10 times. (63 sts)
Rnd 30: K3, M1-k, k28, k1 (ctr-st), k28, M1-k, k3, k9 (stk-sts). (65 sts)
Rnd 31: In Charcoal, p3, M1-k, k29, M1-k, k1 (ctr-st), M1-k, k29, M1-k, p3, k9 (stk-sts). (69 sts)
Rnd 32: In Watermint, k3, p31, k1 (ctr-st), p31, k3, k9 (stk-sts). (69 sts)
Rnd 33: In Charcoal, work as Rnd 31. (73 sts)
Rnd 34: In Charcoal, work as Rnd 32. (73 sts)
Rnd 35: In Watermint, work as Rnd 31. (77 sts)
Rnd 36: In Charcoal, work as Rnd 32. (77 sts)
Rnd 37: In Watermint, work as Rnd 31. (81 sts)
Rnd 38: In Watermint, work as Rnd 32. (81 sts)
Rnd 39: In Watermint, work as Rnd 31. (85 sts)
Rnd 40: In Watermint, work as Rnd 32. (85 sts)
Rnds 41–48: Work as Rnds 31–38. (101 sts)
Rnd 49: In Charcoal, p3, M1-k, k47, work 5 sts into the ctr-st: (k1, yo, k1, yo, k1), k47, M1-k, p3, k9 (stk-sts). (107 sts)
Rnd 50: In Watermint, k3, p48, k1, p1, k1, p1, k1, p48, k3, stk-sts.
Rnd 51: In Charcoal, p3, M1-k, k48, brk1, p1, brk1, p1, brk1, k48, M1-k, k3, stk-sts. (109 sts)

Rnd 52: In Watermint, k3, p49, k1, brp1, k1, brp1, k1, p49, k3, k9 (stk-sts).

Rnd 53: In Charcoal, p3, M1-k, k49, brk1, p1, brk1, p1, brk1, k49, M1-k, k3, k9 (stk-sts). (111 sts)

Rnd 54: In Watermint, k3, p50, k1, brp1, k1, brp1, k1, p50, k3, k9 (stk-sts).

Rnd 55: In Charcoal, p3, M1-k, k50, work 3 sts into the first brioche st: insert right ndl into the leg of the st under the current one and (k1, yo, k1) into it, p1, brk1, p1, work 3 sts into the last brioche st: insert right ndl into the leg of the st under the current one and (k1, yo, k1) into it, k50, M1-k, k3, k9 (stk-sts). (117 sts)

Rnd 56: In Watermint, k3, p51, * k1, brp1 *, rep from * to * 3 times more, k1, p51, k3, k9 (stk-sts).

Rnd 57: In Charcoal, p3, M1-k, k51, * brk1, p1 *, rep from * to * 3 times more, brk1, k51, M1-k, p3, k9 (stk-sts). (119 sts)

Rnd 58: In Watermint, k3, p52, * k1, brp1 *, rep from * to * 3 times more, k1, p52, k3, k9 (stk-sts).

Rnds 59–106: Rep Rnds 55–58 another 12 times. (215 sts)

Rnd 107: In Charcoal, p3, M1-k, k76, 27 sts in brioche patt, k1, M1-k, k11 (ctr-st), M1-k, k1, 27 sts in brioche patt, k76, M1-k, 3 sts garter stitch, k9 (stk-sts). (219 sts)

Rnd 108: In Watermint, k3, p77, 27 sts in brioche patt, p2, k11 (ctr-st), p2, 27 sts in brioche patt, p77, k3, k9 (stk-sts).

Rnds 109–138: Rep Rnds 107–108 another 15 times. (279 sts)

Rnd 139: In Charcoal, p3, M1-k, k92, 27 sts in brioche patt, k17, M1-k, k11 (ctr-st), M1-k, k17, 27 sts in brioche patt, k92, p3, k9 (stk-sts). (283 sts)

Rnd 140: In Watermint, k3, p93, 27 sts in brioche patt, p18, work (k1, yo, k1, yo, k1) into the ctr st, p18, 27 sts in brioche patt, p93, k3, k9 (stk-sts). (287 sts)

Rnd 141: In Charcoal, p3, M1-k, k93, 27 sts in brioche patt, k18, brk1, p1, brk1, p1, brk1, k18, 27 sts in brioche patt, k93, M1-k, p3, k9 (stk-sts). (289 sts)

Rnd 142: In Watermint, k3, p94, 27 sts in brioche patt, p18, k1, brp1, k1, brp1, k1, p18, 27 sts in brioche patt, p94, k3, k9 (stk-sts).

Rnd 143: In Charcoal, 3 sts garter stitch, M1-k, k94, 27 sts in brioche patt, k18, brk1, p1, brk1, p1, brk1, k18, 27 sts in brioche patt, k94, M1-k, 3 sts garter stitch, k9 (stk-sts). (291 sts)

Rnd 144: In Watermint, 3 sts garter stitch, p95, 27 sts in brioche patt, p18, work 3 sts into the first brioche st: insert right ndl into the leg of the st under the current one and (k1, yo, k1) into it, brp1, k1, brp1, work 3 sts into the last brioche st: insert right ndl into the leg of the st under the current one and (k1, yo, k1) into it, p18, 27 sts in brioche patt, p95, 3 sts garter stitch, stk-sts. (295 sts)

Rnds 145–192: Work Rnds 141–144 another 12 times, incorporating increased sts into the patt as follows: at beg and end of rnd, garter stitch, sts before and after (to the left and right of) brioche patt sections in brioche patt. (391 sts)

At the same time, the groups of initially 27 brioche sts are widened after every 6 rnds, 8 times total, by 6 brioche sts to the right and to the left, always toward the outer edge of the shawl; for instance, in the next rnd: P3, M1-k, k89, 33 sts in brioche patt, k18, 9 sts in brioche patt, k18, 33 sts in brioche patt, k89, M1-k, p3, k9 (stk-sts). (297 sts)

In the last rnd, BO the steek sts the regular way, and BO the remaining 391 sts with applied i-cord edging (see p. 23).

FINISHING

Secure the steek as described in Basics (pp. 16–17); then cut it. Fold over the stk-sts to the WS twice, pin, and sew on. Wash the wrap according to the manufacturer's recommendations on the ball band of the yarn, pin it to block, and let it dry. Carefully weave in the remaining ends.

Signe

TWO-COLOR STOLE IN JAPANESE STITCH AND SIMPLE KNIT-PURL PATTERNS

Basics

FINISHED SIZE
67 x 25.6 in (170 x 65 cm)

TOOLS AND MATERIALS
▶ Woll Butt Madeleine (100% wool; 164 yd/150 m, 1.75 oz/50 g per skein); 4 skeins #14230 Off-White and 6 skeins #25346 Mint
▶ Circular knitting needles, US size 4 (3.5 mm), 32–40 in (80–100 cm) long
▶ Stitch markers as needed
▶ Tapestry needle for weaving in ends
▶ Scissors

STITCH PATTERNS
Japanese stitch: See written instructions and chart. The chart shows all rows/rnds and is to be read from right to left. During Rnd 15 only, please note the written instructions—here the first and the last patt rep will be worked slightly differently than the patt reps in between.
Selvedge stitches: Knit.
Steek stitches: Worked as knit sts and not counted in the stitch count.
Ribbing: Alternate "k1-tbl, p1."

GAUGE
In stockinette stitch on US 4 (3.5 mm) needles:
23 sts and 30 rows = 4 x 4 in (10 x 10 cm)

Instructions

CO 147 sts in Off-White.

RIBBING
Row 1: Selv st, * k1-tbl, p1 *, rep from * to * 71 times more, k1-tbl, selv st.
Row 2: Selv st, * p1-tbl, k1 *, rep from * to * 71 times more, p1-tbl, selv st.
CO 9 additional sts for the steek, and join to work in the round.
Rnd 3: Selv st, * k1-tbl, p1 *, rep from * to * 71 times more, k1-tbl, selv st, k9 (stk-sts).
Rnds 4–18: Work as Rnd 3.

FIRST STRIPE BLOCK
Rnd 19: Selv st, k145, selv st, 9 stk-sts.
Rnds 20–24: Work as Rnd 19.
Rnd 25: In Mint, work as Rnd 19.
Rnd 26: K2, * p1, sl1 p-wise wyif *, rep from * to * to 3 sts before the stk-sts, p1, k2, k9 (stk-sts).
Rnds 27–38: In Off-White, work as Rnd 19.
Rnd 39: In Mint, work as Rnd 19.
Rnd 40: K1, p145, k1, k9 (stk-sts).
Rnds 41–52: In Off-White, work as Rnd 19.
Rnd 53: In Mint, work as Rnd 19.
Rnd 54: Work as Rnd 26.
Rnds 55–66: In Off-White, work as Rnd 19.

Rnds 67–150: Work Rnds 39–66 another 3 times.
Rnds 151–164: Work Rnds 39–52 once more.
Rnd 165: In Mint, k all sts, and within this rnd, work k2tog once. (146 sts)

PATTERN BLOCK
Continue in Japanese Stitch patt according to the chart and the following written instructions, working all rnds as: 1 selv st, work the patt rep (18 sts wide) 8 times widthwise, 1 selv st, k9 (stk-sts):
Rnd 1: Selv st, * p2, k1-tbl, p2, k1-tbl, k2tog, yo, k1, yo, skp, k1-tbl, p2, k1-tbl, p2, k1-tbl *, rep from * to * 7 times more, selv st, k9 (stk-sts).
Rnd 2: Selv st, * p2, k1-tbl, p2, k1-tbl, k5, k1-tbl, p2, k1-tbl, p2, k1-tbl *, rep from * to * 7 times more, selv st, k9 (stk-sts).
Rnd 3: Selv st, * p2, k1-tbl, p2, k2tog, yo, k3, yo, skp, p2, k1-tbl, p2, k1-tbl *, rep from * to * 7 times more, selv st, k9 (stk-sts).
Rnd 4: Selv st, * p2, k1-tbl, p2, k7, p2, k1-tbl, p2, k1-tbl *, rep from * to * 7 times more, selv st, k9 (stk-sts).

Rnd 5: Selv st, * p2, k1-tbl, p1, k2tog, yo, k5, yo, skp, p1, k1-tbl, p2, k1-tbl *, rep from * to * 7 times more, selv st, k9 (stk-sts).

Rnd 6: Selv st, * p2, k1-tbl, p1, k9, p1, k1-tbl, p2, k1-tbl *, rep from * to * 7 times more, selv st, k9 (stk-sts).

Rnd 7: Selv st, * p2, k1-tbl, k2tog, yo, k1, k2tog, yo, k1, yo, skp, k1, yo, skp, k1-tbl, p2, k1-tbl *, rep from * to * 7 times more, selv st, k9 (stk-sts).

Rnd 8: Selv st, * p2, k1-tbl, k11, k1-tbl, p2, k1-tbl *, rep from * to * 7 times more, selv st, k9 (stk-sts).

Rnd 9: Selv st, * p2, k2tog, yo, k1, k2tog, yo, k3, yo, skp, k1, yo, skp, p2, k1-tbl *, rep from * to * 7 times more, selv st, k9 (stk-sts).

Rnd 10: Selv st, * p2, k13, p2, k1-tbl *, rep from * to * 7 times more, selv st, k9 (stk-sts).

Rnd 11: Selv st, * p1, k2tog, yo, k1, k2tog, yo, k5, yo, skp, k1, yo, skp, p1, k1-tbl *, rep from * to * 7 times more, selv st, k9 (stk-sts).

Rnd 12: Selv st, * p1, k15, p1, k1-tbl *, rep from * to * 7 times more, selv st, k9 (stk-sts).

Rnd 13: Selv st, * (k2tog, yo, k1) 3 times, (1 yo, skp, k1) 2 times, yo, skp, k1-tbl *, rep from * to * 7 times more, selv st, k9 (stk-sts).

Rnd 14: Selv st, * k17, k1-tbl *, rep from * to * 7 times more, selv st, k9 (stk-sts).

Rnd 15: Selv st, k2, k2tog, yo, k1, k2tog, yo, k3, yo, skp, k1, yo, skp, k1, yo, sk2p, * 1 yo, k1, k2tog, yo, k1, k2tog, yo, k3, yo, skp, k1, yo, skp, k1, yo, sk2p *, rep from * to * 5 times more, yo, k1, k2tog, yo, k1, k2tog, yo, k3, yo, skp, k1, yo, skp, k1, yo, skp, selv st, k9 (stk-sts).

Rnd 16: Selv st, k to last 10 sts, selv st, k9 (stk-sts).

Rnd 17: Selv st, * yo, skp, (k1-tbl, p2) 4 times, k1-tbl, k2tog, yo, k1 *, rep from * to * 7 times more, selv st, k9 (stk-sts).

Rnd 18: Selv st, * (k2, k1-tbl) 5 times, k3 *, rep from * to * 7 times more, selv st, k9 (stk-sts).

Rnd 19: Selv st, * k1, yo, skp, (p2, k1-tbl) 3 times, p2, k2tog, yo, k2 *, rep from * to * 7 times more, selv st, k9 (stk-sts).

Rnd 20: Selv st, * k3, (p2, k1-tbl) 3 times, p2, k4 *, rep from * to * 7 times more, selv st, k9 (stk-sts).

Rnd 21: Selv st, * k2, yo, skp, p1, (k1-tbl, p2) 2 times, k1-tbl, p1, k2tog, yo, k3 *, rep from * to * 7 times more, selv st, k9 (stk-sts).

Rnd 22: Selv st, * k4, p1, (k1-tbl, p2) 2 times, k1-tbl, p1, k5 *, rep from * to * 7 times more, selv st, k9 (stk-sts).

Rnd 23: Selv st, * yo, skp, k1, yo, skp, (k1-tbl, p2) 2 times, k1-tbl, k2tog, yo, k1, k2tog, yo, k1 *, rep from * to * 7 times more, selv st, k9 (stk-sts).

Rnd 24: Selv st, * k5, (k1-tbl, p2) 2 times, k1-tbl, k6 *, rep from * to * 7 times more, selv st, k9 (stk-sts).

Rnd 25: Selv st, * k1, yo, skp, k1, yo, skp, p2, k1-tbl, p2, k2tog, yo, k1, k2tog, yo, k2 *, rep from * to * 7 times more, selv st, k9 (stk-sts).

Rnd 26: Selv st, * k6, p2, k1-tbl, p2, k7 *, rep from * to * 7 times more, selv st, k9 (stk-sts).

Rnd 27: Selv st, * k2, yo, skp, k1, yo, skp, p1, k1-tbl, p1, k2tog, yo, k1, k2tog, yo, k3 *, rep from * to * 7 times more, selv st, k9 (stk-sts).

Rnd 28: Selv st, * k7, p1, k1-tbl, p1, k8 *, rep from * to * 7 times more, selv st, k9 (stk-sts).

Rnd 29: Selv st, * yo, skp, k1, yo, skp, k1, yo, skp, k1-tbl, k2tog, yo, k1, k2tog, yo, k1, k2tog, yo, k1 *, rep from * to * 7 times more, selv st, k9 (stk-sts).

Rnd 30: Selv st, * k8, k1-tbl, k9 *, rep from * to * 7 times more, selv st, stk-sts.

Rnd 31: Selv st, * k1, yo, skp, k1, yo, skp, k1, yo, sk2p, yo, k1, k2tog, yo, k1, skp, yo, k2 *, rep from * to * 7 times more, selv st, k9 (stk-sts).

Rnd 32: Selv st, k to last 10 sts, selv st, k9 (stk-sts).

Rnds 33–128: Work patt Rnds 1–32 another 3 times.

Rnd 129: Selv st, * k1-tbl, p1 *, rep from * to * to selv st, selv st, k9 (stk-sts).

Rnds 130–200: Work 71 rnds more as Rnd 129.

Rnd 201: Selv st, * skp, yo *, rep from * to * to selv st, selv st, k9 (stk-sts).

Rnd 202: Selv st, k all sts and all yo's to last 10 sts, selv st, k9 (stk-sts). Within this rnd, M1-k once. (147 sts)

SECOND STRIPE BLOCK

Rnds 1–12: In Mint, work as Rnd 19 of First Stripe block.

Rnds 13–14: In Off-White, work as Rnds 39–40 of First Stripe block.

Rnds 15–26: In Mint, work as Rnd 19 of First Stripe block.

Rnds 27–28: In Off-White, work as Rnds 25–26 of First Stripe block.

Rnds 29–70: Work Rnds 1–28 once more, and then rep only Rnds 1–14 once.

Rnds 71–76: In Mint, selv st, k to last 10 sts, selv st, k9 (stk-sts).

RIBBING

Rnd 1: Selv st, * k1-tbl, p1 *, rep from * to * 71 times more, k1-tbl, selv st, k9 (stk-sts).

Rnds 2–14: Work as Rnd 1, then BO stk-sts, and continue for 4 more rows in patt. Then BO all sts loosely.

FINISHING

Now, secure the steek as described in Basics (pp. 16–17); then cut it. Fold over the stk-sts to the WS twice, pin, and sew. Wash the stole according to the manufacturer's recommendations on the ball band of the yarn, pin it to block, and let it dry. Carefully weave in the remaining ends.

KNITTING CHART

Refer to key on p. 26.

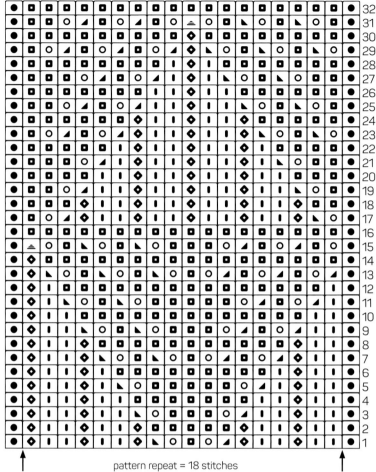

pattern repeat = 18 stitches
work 8 times

Tyra

TRIANGULAR SHAWL IN STRANDED COLORWORK PATTERN

Basics

FINISHED SIZE
63 x 29.9 in (160 x 76 cm)

TOOLS AND MATERIALS
▸ Lang Yarns Baby Alpaca (100% alpaca; 185 yd/169 m, 1.75 oz/50 g per skein); 5 skeins #719.0003 Gray and 3 skeins #719.0080 Purple
▸ Circular knitting needles, 3.0 mm (US size 2 or 3), in different lengths
▸ DPN set, 3.0 mm (US size 2 or 3)
▸ Stitch markers as needed
▸ Scissors
▸ Tapestry needle for weaving in ends

STITCH PATTERNS
The first 4 rows are worked in Gray and have row-by-row instructions. After that, continue in patt according to knitting chart.

Work Rnds 1–16 once, and then rep Rnds 9–16 throughout. The sts at the beginning and at the end of the round always stay the same; just the number of patt reps to be worked in between will increase.
The selvedge st is always worked in Gray. Steek sts are worked alternating colors as follows: 1 st in Purple, 1 st in Gray, 1 st in Purple, 1 st in Gray, 1 st in Purple.

GAUGE
In stockinette stitch on 3.0 mm (US size 2 or 3) needles:
30 sts and 34 rows = 4 x 4 in (10 x 10 cm)

Instructions

CO 4 sts in Gray on DPNs.

Row 1: K1, yo, k2, yo, k1. (6 sts)
Row 2: P1, yo, p-tbl of yo, p2, p-tbl of yo, yo, p1. (8 sts)
Row 3: K1, yo, k-tbl of yo, k4, k-tbl of yo, yo, k1. (10 sts)
Row 4: P1, yo, p-tbl of yo, p6, p-tbl of yo, yo, p1. (12 sts)
After Row 4, CO 5 additional sts for the steek, and join into the round. Now, continue from chart, working Rnds 1–16 once and then rep Rnds 9–16 throughout. Incorporate the increased sts into the patt. In every rnd, after the last patt repeat, the 5 steek sts are always worked alternating colors purple, gray, purple, gray, purple.

Work a total of 220 rounds. (452 sts) Transfer all sts to a spare cord or piece of waste yarn for holding.

KNITTING CHART

Refer to key on p. 26.

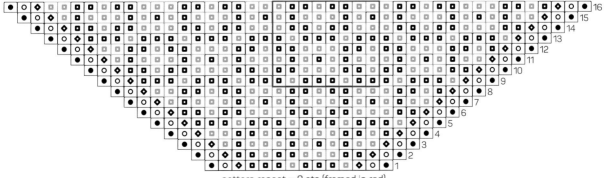

pattern repeat = 8 sts (framed in red)

FINISHING

Now, secure the steek as described in Basics (pp. 16–17); then cut it.

Finish the shawl with a "sandwich" edging. For this, place the 452 formerly held sts on the needle, p/u 168 sts from the nearest side edge, then p/u 1 st from the bottom tip, and then p/u 167 sts from the next side edge. (788 sts)

Work slipped-stitch corners into the sts at the 3 corners (slipped stitch = Rnd 1: k1, Rnd 2: sl-wyib); for shaping, in every rnd, before and after every corner stitch, increase 1 st from the bar between sts in patt (M1-k or M1-p).

Rnd 1: Work 1 slipped stitch, M1-p, * k5, p1 *, rep from * to * to next corner 74 times more, M1-k, work 1 slipped stitch, M1-k, * p1, k5, rep from * to * to next corner 28 times more, M1-p, work 1 slipped stitch, M1-p, * k5, p1 *, rep from * to * to next corner 27 times more, k5, M1-p, work 1 slipped stitch. (794 sts)

Work this round a total of 12 times; then place all sts on holder. (860 sts)

From the wrong side of the shawl, p/u the exact same number of stitches and divide into patt sections as done before. Make sure to divide the patt sections exactly the same way as on the right side of the shawl. Work 12 rounds.

Now, join the border, and bind it off with applied i-cord edging as follows:

With RS of work facing, CO 3 additional sts to the left needle. Slip 1 st from the right needle (WS of work) to the left needle (RS of work), * k2tog, k1, ssk, return these 3 sts to the left needle one after another, and slip 1 st from the right needle to the left needle *, rep from * to * until only 3 sts remain; graft these 3 neatly to the CO edge.

Wash the shawl according to the manufacturer's recommendations on the ball band of the yarn, pin it to block, and let it dry.

Carefully weave in the remaining ends.

Live

CASHMERE SHAWL IN PATTERN MIX

Basics

FINISHED SIZE
82 x 11.8 in (208 x 30 cm)

TOOLS AND MATERIALS
▸ Lang Yarns Cashmere Premium (100% cashmere; 126 yd/115 m, 0.9 oz/25 g per skein); 10 skeins #0028 Lobster
▸ Circular knitting needle, US size 6 (4.0 mm), 16 in (40 cm) long
▸ Circular knitting needle, US size 4 (3.5 mm), 16 in (40 cm) long
▸ Stitch markers as needed
▸ Scissors
▸ Tapestry needle for weaving in ends

STITCH PATTERNS
Stockinette stitch: In rows: knit on RS, purl on WS; in rounds: knit all sts in all rounds.
Selvedge stitches: In rows: knit on RS, purl on WS; in rounds: knit all selv sts in all rounds.
Steek stitches: Worked as knit sts and not counted in the stitch count.

GAUGE
In stockinette stitch on US 6 (4.0 mm) needles:
22 sts and 34 rows = 4 x 4 in (10 x 10 cm)

Instructions

Using US 6 (4.0 mm) needle, CO 64 sts, and work zigzag edging as follows:
Rows 1–6: Selv st, 62 sts in stockinette stitch, selv st.
Row 7: Selv st, * skp, yo *, rep from * to * 30 times more, selv st.
Row 8: Selv st, p62, selv st.
Rows 9–14: Selv st, 62 sts in stockinette stitch, selv st.
Now, using a spare circular in size US 4 (3.5 mm), insert needle into every stitch of the CO row sts. Hold the spare needle with the picked-up sts parallel behind the main needle, and knit the sts from both needles together in pairs: always 1 st from the front needle with 1 st from the back needle.
CO 9 additional sts for the steek, and join into the round.
Rnds 1–2: P1, k3, * k2, p8, k2, p2 *, rep from * to * 3 times more, k3, p1, k9 (stk-sts).
Rnds 3–4: P1, k3, * k8, p2, k2, p2 *, rep from * to * 3 times more, k3, p1, k9 (stk-sts).
Rnds 5–6: P1, k3, * p6, k2, p2, k2, p2 *, rep from * to * 3 times more, k3, p1, k9 (stk-sts).
Rnds 7–8: P1, k3, * k4, p2, k2, p2, k4 *, rep from * to * 3 times more, p1, k9 (stk-sts).

Rnds 9–10: P1, k3, * p2, k2, p2, k2, p6 *, rep from * to * 3 times more, k3, p1, k9 (stk-sts).
Rnds 11–12: P1, k3, * p2, k2, p2, k8 *, rep from * to * 3 times more, k3, p1, k9 (stk-sts).
Rnds 13–14: P1, k3, * p2, k2, p8, k2 *, rep from * to * 3 times more, k3, p1, k9 (stk-sts).
Rnds 15–16: P1, k3, * p2, k8, p2, k2 *, rep from * to * 3 times more, k3, p1, k9 (stk-sts).
Rnds 17–18: P1, k3, * p8, k2, p2, k2 *, rep from * to * 3 times more, k3, p1, k9 (stk-sts).
Rnds 19–20: P1, k3, * k6, p2, k2, p2, k2 *, rep from * to * 3 times more, k3, p1, k9 (stk-sts).
Rnds 21–22: P1, k3, * p4, k2, p2, k2, p4 *, rep from * to * 3 times more, k3, p1, k9 (stk-sts).
Rnds 23–24: P1, k3, * k2, p2, k2, p2, k6 *, rep from * to * 3 times more, k3, p1, k9 (stk-sts).
Rnds 25–26: P1, k3, * k2, p2, k2, p8 *, rep from * to * 3 times more, k3, p1, k9 (stk-sts).
Rnds 27–28: P1, k3, * k2, p2, k8, p2 *, rep from * to * 3 times more, k3, p1, k9 (stk-sts).

Rnds 29–112: Work Rnds 1–28 another 3 times.

Rnds 113–115: P1, k3, p56, k3, p1, k9 (stk-sts).

Rnd 116: P1, k3, * k2, yo, skp, k4 *, rep from * to * 6 times more, k3, p1, k9 (stk-sts).

Rnd 117 and all other odd-numbered rounds: P1, k62, p1, k9 (stk-sts).

Rnd 118: P1, k3, * k3, yo, skp, k3 *, rep from * to * 6 times more, k3, p1, k9 (stk-sts).

Rnd 120: P1, k3, * k4, yo, skp, k2 *, rep from * to * 6 times more, k3, p1, k9 (stk-sts).

Rnd 122: P1, k3, * yo, skp, k6 *, rep from * to * 6 times more, k3, p1, k9 (stk-sts).

Rnd 124: P1, k3, * k1, yo, skp, k5 *, rep from * to * 6 times more, k3, p1, k9 (stk-sts).

Rnd 126: P1, k3, * k2, yo, skp, k4 *, rep from * to * 6 times more, k3, p1, k9 (stk-sts).

Rnd 128: P1, k3, * k6, yo, skp *, rep from * to * 6 times more, k3, p1, k9 (stk-sts).

Rnd 130: P1, k2, * yo, skp, k6 *, rep from * to * 6 times more, k4, p1, k9 (stk-sts).

Rnd 132: P1, k3, * yo, skp, k6 *, rep from * to * 6 times more, k3, p1, k9 (stk-sts).

Rnd 134: P1, k3, * k4, yo, skp, k2 *, rep from * to * 6 times more, k3, p1, k9 (stk-sts).

Rnd 136: P1, k3, * k5, yo, skp, k1 *, rep from * to * 6 times more, k3, p1, k9 (stk-sts).

Rnd 138: P1, k3, * k6, yo, skp *, rep from * to * 6 times more, k3, p1, k9 (stk-sts).

Rnds 140–142: P1, k3, p56, k3, p1, k9 (stk-sts).

Rnds 143–154: P1, k3, * k2, p2 *, rep from * to * 13 times more, k3, p1, 9 stk-sts.

Rnds 155–166: P1, k3, * p2, k2 *, rep from * to * 13 times more, k3, p1, 9 stk-sts.

Rnds 167–178: Work as Rnds 143–154.

Rnds 179–190: Work as Rnds 155–166.

Rnds 191–202: Work as Rnds 143–154.

Rnds 203–214: Work as Rnds 155–166.

Rnds 215–226: Work as Rnds 143–154.

Rnds 227–229: Work as Rnds 140–142.

Rnds 230–253: Work as Rnds 116–139.

Rnds 254–373: Rep last 24 rnds 5 times more.

Rnds 374–376: Work as Rnds 140–142.

Rnds 377–460: Work as Rnds 143–226.

Rnds 461–463: Work as Rnds 140–142.

Rnds 464–487: Work as Rnds 116–139.

Rnds 488–490: Work as Rnds 140–142.

Rnds 491–602: Work Rnds 1–28 4 times, binding off the stk-sts in the last rnd, and continue in rows.

EDGING

Finish off with zigzag edging as follows:

Rows 1–6: Selv st, 62 sts in stockinette stitch, selv st.

Row 7: Selv st, * skp, yo *, rep from * to * 30 times more, selv st.

Row 8: Selv st, p62, selv st.

Rows 9–14: Selv st, 62 sts in stockinette stitch, selv st.

Now, using a spare circular in size US 4 (3.5 mm) in the first row of stockinette, from the back of the work, insert the needle into every stitch, and let the sts slide onto the spare needle. Hold the spare needle with the picked-up sts parallel behind the main needle, and knit the sts from both needles together in pairs: always 1 st from the front needle with 1 st from the back needle.

FINISHING

Secure the steek as described in Basics (pp. 16–17); then cut it. Fold over the stk-sts to the WS twice, pin, and sew on. Wash the stole according to the manufacturer's recommendations on the ball band of the yarn, pin it to block, and let it dry. Carefully weave in the remaining ends.

Lilja

TRIANGULAR SHAWL IN RIPPLE PATTERN

Basics

FINISHED SIZE
82.7 x 28.3 in (210 x 72 cm)

TOOLS AND MATERIALS
▶ Rowan Alpaca Soft DK (70% wool, 30% alpaca; 136 yd/125 m, 1.75 oz/50 g per skein); 7 skeins #202 Trench Coat
▶ Circular knitting needles, US size 6 (4.0 mm) in different lengths
▶ DPN set, US size 6 (4.0 mm)
▶ Stitch markers as needed
▶ Scissors
▶ Tapestry needle for weaving in ends

STITCH PATTERNS
Ripple pattern: See written instructions and chart. Shown are the first few rows and one patt repeat, which needs to be continued as established. The chart is to be read from right to left for RS rows. For a better overview, stitches are shown as they appear on the right side of work (public side of the shawl). This means that WS rows have to be read from left to right. Stitches shown in the chart as "knit" for WS rows have to be purled in WS rows, and vice versa. In the written-out, row-by-row instructions, sts are named as they have to be worked (i.e., if to be knit, written instructions will state "knit").
Selvedge stitches: In rows: knit on RS, purl on WS; in rounds: knit all selv sts in all rounds.
Steek stitches: Worked as knit sts and not counted in the stitch count.

GAUGE
In stockinette stitch on US 6 (4.0 mm) needles:
22 sts and 30 rows = 4 x 4 in (10 x 10 cm)

Instructions

CO 4 sts, work 1 WS row in purl.
Row 1: Selv st, yo, k2, yo, selv st. (6 sts)
Row 2: Selv st, yo, p-tbl of yo, p2, p-tbl of yo, yo, selv st. (8 sts)
Row 3: Selv st, yo, k-tbl of yo, k4, k-tbl of yo, yo, selv st. (10 sts)
Row 4: Selv st, yo, p-tbl of yo, p6, p-tbl of yo, yo, selv st. (12 sts)
Row 5: Selv st, yo, k-tbl of yo, k8, k-tbl of yo, yo, selv st. (14 sts)
Row 6: Selv st, yo, p-tbl of yo, p10, p-tbl of yo, yo, selv st.
CO 4 additional sts for the steek, distribute sts onto a DPN set, and join into the round. (16 sts)
Rnd 7: Selv st, yo, k-tbl of yo, p1, k1, yo, k1, yo, k1, yo, k1, skp 3 times, p1, k-tbl of yo, yo, selv st, 4 stk-sts. (18 sts)
Rnd 8 and all other even-numbered rounds, unless described otherwise: Selv st, yo, k-tbl or p-tbl of yo in patt, work the following sts as they appear, working k-tbl into the yo's, and working the yo before the selv st in patt as k-tbl or p-tbl, yo, selv st, k4 (stk-sts). (20 sts)
Rnd 9: Selv st, yo, k-tbl of yo, k2, p1, k2, yo, k1, yo, k1, yo, skp 3 times, p1, k2, k-tbl of yo, yo, selv st, k4 (stk-sts). (22 sts)
Rnd 11: Selv st, yo, k-tbl of yo, k4, p1, k1, yo, k1, yo, k1, yo, k1, skp 3 times, p1, k4, k-tbl of yo, yo, selv st, k4 (stk-sts). (26 sts)
Rnd 13: Selv st, yo, k-tbl of yo, k6, p1, k2, yo, k1, yo, k1, yo, skp 3 times, p1, k6, k-tbl of yo, yo, selv st, k4 (stk-sts). (30 sts)
Rnd 15: Selv st, yo, k-tbl of yo, k8, p1, k1, yo, k1, yo, k1, yo, k1, skp 3 times, p1, k8, k-tbl of yo, yo, selv st, k4 (stk-sts). (34 sts)
Rnd 17: Selv st, yo, k-tbl of yo, k10, p1, k10, p1, k10, k-tbl of yo, yo, selv st, k4 (stk-sts). (38 sts)
Rnd 18: Selv st, yo, k-tbl of yo, p1, k10, p1, k10, p1, k10, p1, k-tbl of yo, yo, selv st, k4 (stk-sts). (40 sts)
Rnd 19: Selv st, yo, k-tbl of yo, k1, p1, k10, p1, k10, p1, k10, p1, k1, k-tbl of yo, yo, selv st, k4 (stk-sts). (42 sts)
Rnd 20: Selv st, yo, k-tbl of yo, k2, p1, k10, p1, k10, p1, k10, p1, k2, k-tbl of yo, yo, selv st, k4 (stk-sts). (44 sts)
Rnd 21: Selv st, yo, k-tbl of yo, k3, * p1, k2tog 3 times, k1, yo, k1, yo, k1, yo, k1 *,

rep from * to * 2 times more, p1, k3, k-tbl of yo, yo, selv st, k4 (stk-sts). (46 sts)

Rnd 23: Selv st, yo, k-tbl of yo, k5, * p1, k2tog 3 times, yo, k1, yo, k1, yo, k2 *, rep from * to * 2 times more, p1, k5, k-tbl of yo, yo, selv st, k4 (stk-sts). (50 sts)

Rnd 25: Selv st, yo, k-tbl of yo, k7, * p1, k2tog 3 times, k1, yo, k1, yo, k1, yo, k1 *, rep from * to * 2 times more, p1, k7, k-tbl of yo, yo, selv st, k4 (stk-sts). (54 sts)

Rnd 27: Selv st, yo, k-tbl of yo, k9, * p1, k2tog 3 times, yo, k1, yo, k1, yo, k2 *, rep from * to * 2 times more, p1, k9, k-tbl of yo, yo, selv st, k4 (stk-sts). (58 sts)

Rnd 29: Selv st, yo, k-tbl of yo, p1, k10, * p1, k2tog 3 times, k1, yo, k1, yo, k1, yo, k1 *, rep from * to * 2 times more, p1, k10, p1, k-tbl of yo, yo, selv st, k4 (stk-sts). (62 sts)

Rnd 31: Selv st, yo, k-tbl of yo, k2, * p1, k10 *, rep from * to * 4 times more, p1, k2, k-tbl of yo, yo, selv st, k4 (stk-sts). (66 sts)

Rnd 32: Selv st, yo, k-tbl of yo, k3, * p1, k10 *, rep from * to * 4 times more, p1, k3, k-tbl of yo, yo, selv st, k4 (stk-sts). (68 sts)

Rnd 33: Selv st, yo, k-tbl of yo, k4, * p1, k10 *, rep from * to * 4 times more, p1, k4, k-tbl of yo, yo, selv st, k4 (stk-sts). (70 sts)

Rnd 34: Selv st, yo, k-tbl of yo, k5, * p1, k10 *, rep from * to * 4 times more, p1, k5, k-tbl of yo, yo, selv st, k4 (stk-sts). (72 sts)

Rnds 35–142: Work Rnds 7–34 another 3 times; then rep only Rnds 7–30 once, incorporating increased sts into the patt and, every time 11 sts have accumulated before or after the twisted yo's, working a complete patt rep more.

Rnds 143–165: Work Rnd 31 another 23 times, but modify the patt rep to: p1, k4, p1, k6.

Rnds 166–201: Work Rnds 7–30 once, taking care to divide into patt reps the same way as in the bottom part of the shawl.

After having completed the last round, BO the 4 stk-sts, and finish work in back-and forth rows.

Knit 1 row, turn work, and BO all sts on the WS.

FINISHING

Now, secure the steek as described in Basics (pp. 16–17); then cut it. P/u sts from the side edge of the steek as follows: * from the next 3 selv-sts, p/u 1 st each, skip 1 st *, rep from * to * to the end of this side, work 7 rows in stockinette stitch, BO all sts loosely; then fold over to the WS, pin in place, and sew on. Finish the second edge the same way.

Wash the shawl according to the manufacturer's recommendations on the ball band of the yarn, pin it to block, and let it dry.

Carefully weave in the remaining ends.

KNITTING CHART

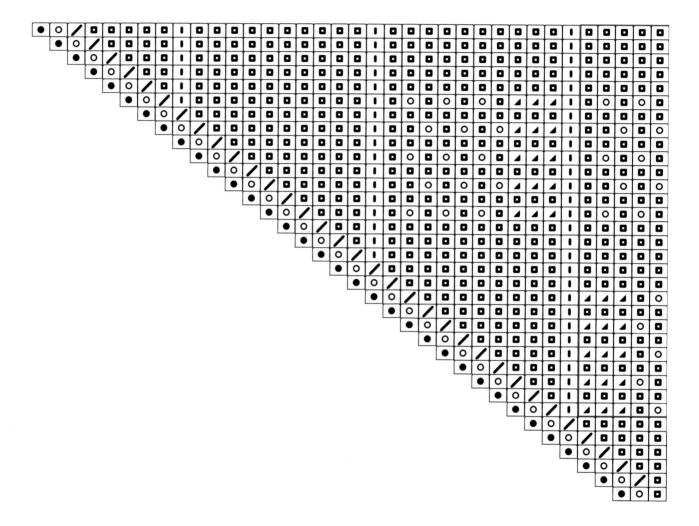

Refer to key on p. 26.

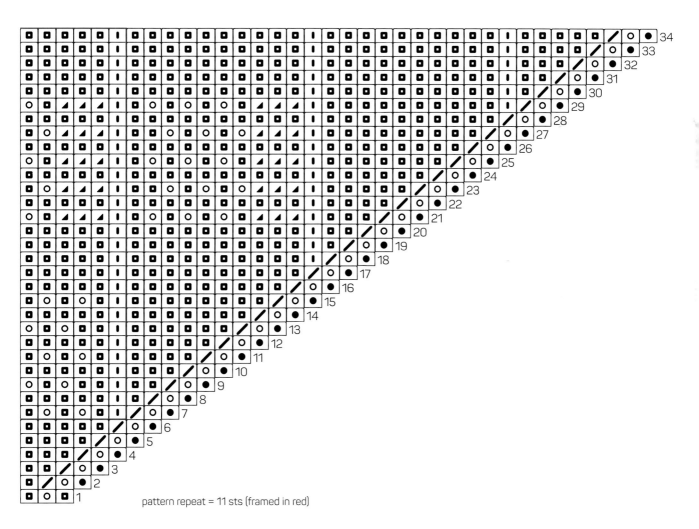

pattern repeat = 11 sts (framed in red)

Svea

TRIANGULAR SHAWL WITH SLIPPED STITCHES AND A WIDE BORDER

Basics

FINISHED SIZE
78.8 x 27.6 in (200 x 70 cm)

TOOLS AND MATERIALS
▶ Lang Yarns Merino 150 (100% wool; 164 yd/150 m, 1.75 oz/50 g per skein); 5 skeins #29 Watermelon or #162 Burgundy and 4 skeins #124 Mouse Gray
▶ Circular knitting needles, US size 4 (3.5 mm) in different lengths
▶ DPN set, US size 4 (3.5 mm)
▶ Stitch markers as needed
▶ Scissors
▶ Tapestry needle for weaving in ends

GAUGE
In stockinette stitch on US 4 (3.5 mm) needles:
27 sts and 37 rows = 4 x 4 in (10 x 10 cm)

STITCH PATTERNS
Work from charts. Chart #1 shows Rnds 1–25; work these once, and then rep Rnds 14–25 only (= 1 height-wise patt rep). The first and the last sts are always worked the same in every rnd; only the patt rep (highlighted in blue) is worked widthwise by 2 reps more often per height-wise patt rep (= after 13 rnds, 1 patt rep; after 25 rnds, 3 patt reps, etc.). The chart is read from right to left.

The chart for the border applies to working in the round as well as in rows. Stitches are shown in the chart as they appear on the right side of work (public side of the shawl). This means that for the border, when working in rows, the WS rows of the chart have to be read from left to right. Stitches shown as "knit" for WS rows have to be purled in WS rows, and vice versa, and decreases shown as ssk have to be worked as ssp. In the written-out instructions for the border, all sts are listed exactly as they are to be worked (i.e., sts to be knit are listed as "knit").
Steek stitches: Worked as knit sts and not counted in the stitch count.

Instructions

CO 12 sts in Mouse Gray, distribute the sts onto a DPN set, and join into the round.
WS row: P the selv st, yo, p10, yo, p the selv st. (14 sts).
Work the next RS row in either Watermelon or in Burgundy: K the selv st, yo, k-tbl of yo, k10, k-tbl of yo, yo, k the selv st. (16 sts)
After having completed this row, CO 9 additional sts for the steek, join to work in the round, and distribute the sts evenly onto a DPN set.

From here on, continue working in the round, always alternating 1 rnd in Burgundy or Watermelon with 1 rnd in Mouse Gray. Increases at the sides are worked in every rnd as follows:
Basic increase: Selv st, yo, k-tbl of yo, work in patt to the last 2 sts of the rnd, k-tbl of yo, yo, selv st, k9 (stk-sts).
First, work Rnds 1–25 of the chart once; then work Rnds 14–25 another 20 times. (546 sts)
Then work the border in Watermelon or Burgundy without further increases.

BORDER
Please also refer to Chart #2.
Rnd 1: Selv st, * k2, yo, skp, ssk, (k1, yo) 8 times, k1, k2tog *, rep from * to * 31 times more, selv st, k9 (stk-sts). (738 sts)
Rnd 2: Selv st, * k2tog, yo, k2, ssk, k15, k2tog *, rep from * to * 31 times more, selv st, k9 (stk-sts). (674 sts)
Rnd 3: Selv st, * k2, yo, skp, ssk, k13, k2tog *, rep from * to * 31 times more, selv st, k9 (stk-sts). (610 sts)
Rnd 4: Selv st, * k2tog, yo, k2, ssk, k11, k2tog *, rep from * to * 31 times more, selv st, k9 (stk-sts). (546 sts)
Repeat these 4 rnds until a height of 3.15 in (8 cm) has been reached. In Rnd 4 of the patt, BO the 9 stk-sts, and then work another 4 rows for the border as follows:

Row 1: Selv st, * k2, yo, skp, ssk, (k1, yo) 8 times, k1, k2tog *, rep from * to * 31 times more, selv st. (738 sts)

Row 2: Selv st, * p2tog, yo, p2, ssp, p15, p2tog *, rep from * to * 31 times more, selv st. (674 sts)

Row 3: Selv st, * k2, yo, skp, ssk, k13, k2tog *, rep from * to * 31 times more, selv st. (610 sts)

Row 4: Selv st, * p2tog, yo, p2, ssp, p11, p2tog *, rep from * to * 31 times more, selv st. (546 sts)

Afterward, BO all sts with applied i-cord edging (see p. 23).

FINISHING

Secure the steek as described in Basics (pp. 16–17); then cut it.

Fold over the stk-sts to the WS twice, pin, and sew on.

Wash the wrap according to the manufacturer's recommendations on the ball band of the yarn, pin it to block, and let it dry.

Carefully weave in the remaining ends.

CHART #2: BORDER

Refer to key on p. 26.

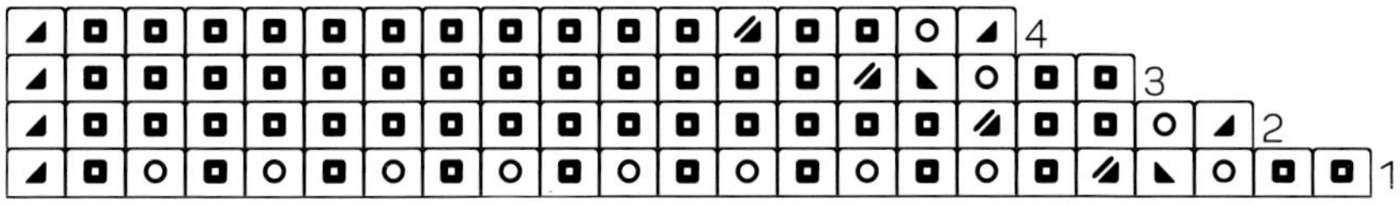

Please note

The large image shows the shawl worked with Burgundy as the main color. Watermelon as the main color is shown in the smaller pictures.

CHART #1

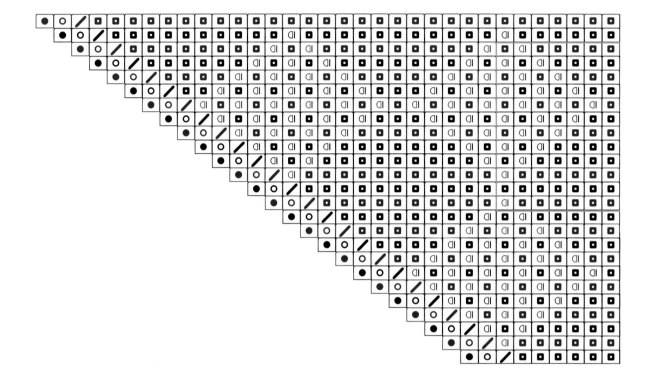

Refer to key on p. 26.

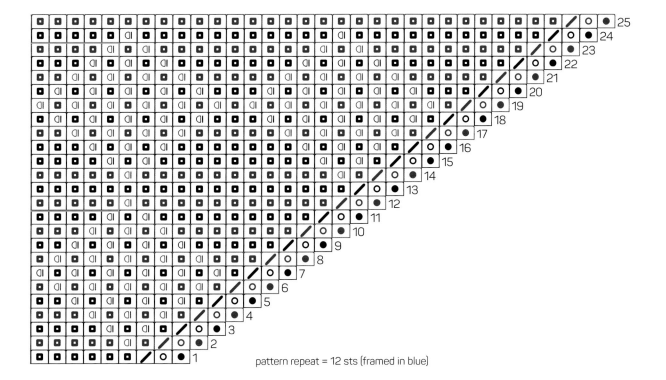

pattern repeat = 12 sts (framed in blue)

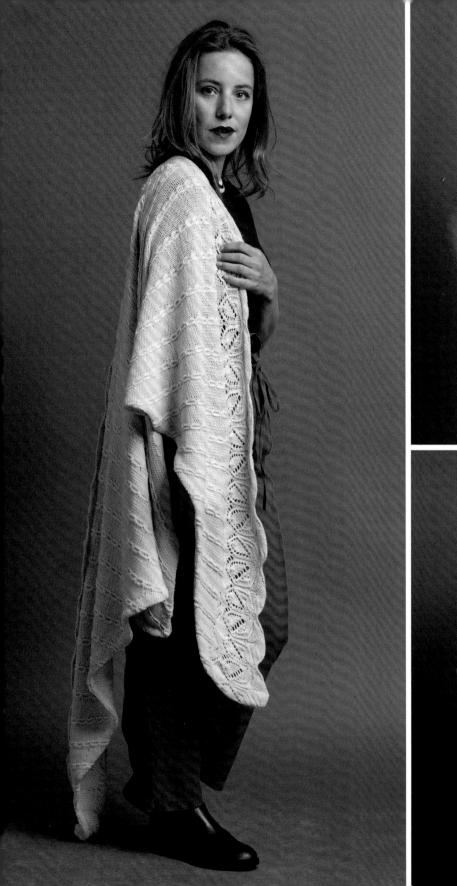

BIG TRIANGULAR SHAWL IN JAPANESE STITCH

Basics

FINISHED SIZE
82.7 x 37.4 in (210 x 95 cm)

TOOLS AND MATERIALS
▷ Woll Butt Madeleine (100% wool; 164 yd/150 m, 1.75 oz/50 g per skein); 11 skeins #28620 Apricot
▷ Circular knitting needles, US size 4 (3.5 mm) in different lengths
▷ DPN set, US size 4 (3.5 mm)
▷ Stitch markers as needed
▷ Scissors
▷ Tapestry needle for weaving in ends

STITCH PATTERNS
Selvedge stitches: In RS rows, k the first and the last st of the row; in WS rows, p the first and the last st of the row.

Japanese Stitch Border: See written instructions and chart. The chart shows one patt rep, which is repeated 23 times widthwise per round. All rounds are shown in the chart. The chart is to be read from right to left. All sts are shown as they appear on the right side of work (public side of the shawl).

Mini cable: Insert the right needle into the 3rd stitch on the left needle and pass it to the right, over the 2nd and 1st sts, and off the needle; knit the 1st st, yo, knit the 2nd st.

Steek stitches: Worked as knit sts and not counted in the stitch count.

GAUGE
In stockinette stitch on US 4 (3.5 mm) needles:
23 sts and 30 rows = 4 x 4 in (10 x 10 cm)

Instructions

The shawl is worked from the long edge toward the tip.
CO 462 sts.

Row 1 (WS): Purl all sts.

Row 2: Selv st, * k5, p9, k5, p1 *, rep from * to * 22 times more, selv st.
CO 9 additional sts for the steek, distribute the sts onto a DPN set, and join into the round.

Rnd 3: Selv st, * yo, k2, skp, k1, p9, k1, k2tog, k2, yo, p1 *, rep from * to * 22 times more, selv st, k9 (stk-sts).

Rnd 4: Selv st, * k1, yo, k2, skp, p9, k2tog, k2, yo, k1, p1 *, rep from * to * 22 times more, selv st, k9 (stk-sts).

Rnd 5: Selv st, * k2, yo, k2, skp, p7, k2tog, k2, yo, k2, p1 *, rep from * to * 22 times more, selv st, k9 (stk-sts).

Rnd 6: Selv st, * k3, yo, k2, skp, p5, k2tog, k2, yo, k3, p1 *, rep from * to * 22 times more, selv st, k9 (stk-sts).

Rnd 7: Selv st, * k4, yo, k2, skp, p3, k2tog, k2, yo, k4, p1 *, rep from * to * 22 times more, selv st, k9 (stk-sts).

Rnd 8: Selv st, * k5, yo, k2, skp, p1, k2tog, k2, yo, k5, p1 *, rep from * to * 22 times more, selv st, k9 (stk-sts).

Rnd 9: Selv st, * yo, k2, skp, k5, p1, k5, k2tog, k2, yo, p1 *, rep from * to * 22 times more, selv st, k9 (stk-sts).

Rnd 10: Selv st, * k1, yo, k2, skp, k4, p1, k4, k2tog, k2, yo, k1, p1 *, rep from * to * 22 times more, selv st, k9 (stk-sts).

Rnd 11: Selv st, * k2, yo, k2, skp, k3, p1, k3, k2tog, k2, yo, k2, p1 *, rep from * to * 22 times more, selv st, k9 (stk-sts).

Rnd 12: Selv st, * k3, yo, k2, skp, k2, p1, k2, k2tog, k2, yo, k3, p1 *, rep from * to * 22 times more, selv st, k9 (stk-sts).

Rnd 13: Selv st, * k4, yo, k2, skp, k1, p1, k1, k2tog, k2, yo, k4, p1 *, rep from * to * 22 times, selv st, k9 (stk-sts).

Rnd 14: Selv st, * k5, yo, k2, skp, p1, k2tog, k2, yo, k5, p1 *, rep from * to * 22 times more, selv st, k9 (stk-sts).

Rnd 15: Selv st, * k2, yo, skp, (k1-tbl, p1) 5 times, k1-tbl, k2tog, yo, k2, p1 *, rep from * to * 22 times more, selv st, k9 (stk-sts).

Rnd 16: Selv st, * k4, (k1-tbl, p1) 5 times, k1-tbl, k4, p1 *, rep from * to * 22 times more, selv st, k9 (stk-sts).

Rnd 17: Selv st, * skp, yo, k1, yo, skp, (p1, k1-tbl) 4 times, p1, k2tog, yo, k1, yo, k2tog, p1 *, rep from * to * 22 times more, selv st, k9 (stk-sts).

Rnd 18: Selv st, * k5, (p1, k1-tbl) 4 times, p1, k5, p1 *, rep from * to * 22 times more, selv st, k9 (stk-sts).

Rnd 19: Selv st, * skp, yo, k2, yo, skp, (k1-tbl, p1) 3 times, k1-tbl, k2tog, yo, k2, yo, k2tog, p1 *, rep from * to * 22 times more, selv st, k9 (stk-sts).

Rnd 20: Selv st, * k6, (k1-tbl, p1) 3 times, k1-tbl, k6, p1 *, rep from * to * 22 times more, selv st, k9 (stk-sts).

Rnd 21: Selv st, * skp, yo, k3, yo, skp, (p1, k1-tbl) 2 times, p1, k2tog, yo, k3, yo, k2tog, p1 *, rep from * to * 22 times more, selv st, k9 (stk-sts).

Rnd 22: Selv st, * k7, (p1, k1-tbl) 2 times, p1, k7, p1 *, rep from * to * 22 times more, selv st, k9 (stk-sts).

Rnd 23: Selv st, * skp, yo, k4, yo, skp, k1-tbl, p1, k1-tbl, k2tog, yo, k4, yo, k2tog, p1 *, rep from * to * 22 times more, selv st, k9 (stk-sts).

Rnd 24: Selv st, * k8, k1-tbl, p1, k1-tbl, k8, p1 *, rep from * to * 22 times more, selv st, k9 (stk-sts).

Rnd 25: Selv st, * skp, yo, k5, yo, skp, p1, k2tog, yo, k5, yo, k2tog, p1 *, rep from * to * 22 times more, selv st, k9 (stk-sts).

Rnd 26: Selv st, * k9, p1, k9, p1 *, rep from * to * 22 times more, selv st, 9 stk-sts.

Rnd 27: Selv st, * yo, skp, yo, k1, sk2p, k1, yo, k2tog, yo, p1, yo, skp, yo, k1, sk2p, k1, yo, k2tog, yo, p1 *, rep from * to * 22 times more, selv st, k9 (stk-sts).

Rnd 28: Selv st, * k8, p3, k8, p1 *, rep from * to * 22 times more, selv st, k9 (stk-sts).

Rnd 29: Selv st, * k1, yo, skp, yo, sk2p, yo, k2tog, yo, p3, yo, skp, yo, sssk (see Abbreviations), yo, k2tog, yo, k1, p1 *, rep from * to * 22 times more, selv st, k9 (stk-sts).

Rnd 30: Selv st, * k7, p5, k7, p1 *, rep from * to * 22 times more, selv st, k9 (stk-sts).

Rnd 31: Selv st, * k2, yo, skp, k1, k2tog, yo, p5, yo, skp, k1, k2tog, yo, k2, p1 *, rep from * to * 22 times more, selv st, k9 (stk-sts).

Rnd 32: Selv st, * k6, p7, k6, p1 *, rep from * to * 22 times more, selv st, k9 (stk-sts).

Rnd 33: Selv st, * k3, yo, sk2p, yo, p7, yo, sk2p, yo, k3, p1 *, rep from * to * 22 times more, selv st, k9 (stk-sts).

Rnd 34: Selv st, * k5, p9, k5, p1 *, rep from * to * 22 times more, selv st, k9 (stk-sts).

Rnd 35: Selv st, * yo, k2, skp, k1, p9, k1, k2tog, k2, yo, p1 *, rep from * to * 22 times more, selv st, k9 (stk-sts).

Rnd 36: Selv st, * k1, yo, k2, skp, p9, k2tog, k2, yo, k1, p1 *, rep from * to * 22 times more, selv st, k9 (stk-sts).

Rnd 37: Selv st, * k2, yo, k2, skp, p7, k2tog, k2, yo, k2, p1 *, rep from * to * 22 times more, selv st, k9 (stk-sts).

Rnd 38: Selv st, * k3, yo, k2, skp, p5, k2tog, k2, yo, k3, p1 *, rep from * to * 22 times more, selv st, k9 (stk-sts).

Rnd 39: Selv st, *k4, yo, k2, skp, p3, k2tog, k2, yo, k4, p1 *, rep from * to * 22 times more, selv st, k9 (stk-sts).

Rnd 40: Selv st, * k5, yo, k2, skp, p1, k2tog, k2, yo, k5, p1 *, rep from * to * 22 times more, selv st, k9 (stk-sts).

Rnd 41: Selv st, * skp, yo *, rep from * to * to next selv st, k9 (stk-sts).

Now, at the beginning of every round, you will p2tog the 2 sts after the selv st; at the end of the round, p2tog the 2 sts before the selv st.

Rnd 42: Selv st, p2tog, * p7, k1-tbl, p1, k1-tbl *, rep from * to * to 8 sts before the selv st, p6, p2tog, selv st, k9 (stk-sts). (460 sts)

Rnds 43–46: Work as Rnd 42. (452 sts)

Rnd 47: Selv st, p2tog, p2, mini cable over 3 sts, * p7, mini cable over 3 sts *, rep from * to * to 3 sts before the selv st, p1, p2tog, selv st, k9 (stk-sts). (450 sts)

Rep Rnds 42–47 continuously until only 12 sts remain on the needles. BO the 9 stk-sts and continue in turned rows. Continue to work decreases in every row. When only 4 sts remain, BO all sts.

FINISHING

Now, secure the steek as described in Basics (pp. 16–17); then cut it. Fold over the stk-sts to the WS twice, pin, and sew on. Wash the wrap according to the manufacturer's recommendations on the ball band of the yarn, pin it to block, and let it dry. Carefully weave in the remaining ends.

CHART #1: JAPANESE STITCH

Refer to key on p. 26.

pattern repeat = 20 sts
work 23 times

CHART #2: MINI CABLE PATTERN

SEMICIRCULAR SHAWL WITH LACE STRIP AND ZIGZAG BORDER

Basics

FINISHED SIZE
86.6 x 22.5 in (220 x 57 cm)

TOOLS AND MATERIALS
▶ Amano Yarns Awa (55% baby alpaca, 26% merino wool, 19% pima cotton; 328 yd/300 m, 3.5 oz/100 g per skein); 2 skeins #1101 Honey and 1 skein #1109 Red Berry
▶ Circular knitting needles, US size 6 (4.0 mm) in different lengths
▶ DPN set, US size 6 (4.0 mm)
▶ Stitch markers as needed
▶ Scissors
▶ Tapestry needle for weaving in ends

STITCH PATTERNS
Seed stitch: Row/Rnd 1: alternate k1, p1; Row/Rnd 2: alternate p1, k1.

Garter stitch: In rows: knit all sts in all rows; in rounds, alternate—Rnd 1: knit; Rnd 2: purl.

Lace pattern / Lace border: See instructions.

Steek stitches: Worked as knit sts and not counted in the stitch count.

Brioche knit (brk): Rnd 1: k1; Rnd 2: insert the right needle from front to back into the stitch 1 rnd below the st to be worked, pull the working yarn through this st, and lift it onto the right needle. This dissolves the st above and places it like a yarn over, onto the needle.

Brioche purl (brp): Rnd 1: p1; Rnd 2: insert the right needle from back to front into the stitch 1 rnd below the st to be worked, pull the working yarn through this st, and lift it onto the right needle. This dissolves the st above and places it like a yarn over, onto the needle.

GAUGE
In stockinette stitch on US 6 (4.0 mm) needles:
22 sts and 28 rows = 4 x 4 in (10 x 10 cm)

Instructions

CO 5 sts in Honey.
Row 1: K2, p1, k2.
Row 2: P1, yo, p1, k1, p1, yo, p1. (7 sts)
Row 3: K1, yo, p-tbl of yo, k1, p1, k1, p-tbl of yo, yo, k1. (9 sts)
Row 4: P1, yo, k-tbl of yo, 5 sts in seed stitch, k-tbl of yo, yo, p1. (11 sts)
Row 5: K1, yo, p-tbl of yo, 7 sts in seed stitch, p-tbl of yo, yo, k1. (13 sts)
Row 6: P1, yo, k-tbl of yo, 9 sts in seed stitch, k-tbl of yo, yo, p1. (15 sts)
After this row, CO 4 additional sts for the steek, join to work in the round, and distribute sts onto a DPN set.
Rnd 7: K1, yo, k-tbl of yo, 11 sts in seed stitch, k-tbl of yo, yo, k1, k4 (stk-sts). (17 sts)

Rnds 8–72: Work 65 rnds more as Rnd 7. (147 sts)

Rnd 73: In Red Berry, k1, yo, k-tbl of yo, k all sts, k-tbl of yo, yo, k1, k4 (stk-sts). (149 sts)

Rnd 74: K1, yo, p-tbl of yo, p all sts, p-tbl of yo, yo, k1, k4 (stk-sts). (151 sts)

Rnds 75–76: In Honey, work as Rnds 73–74. (155 sts)

Rnds 77–79: In Red Berry, work as Rnds 73–74. (159 sts)

LACE STRIPS IN OPENWORK PATTERN WITH TRIANGLES

Rnds 1–4: In Honey, k1, yo, k-tbl or p-tbl of yo in patt, 157 sts garter stitch, k-tbl or p-tbl of yo in patt, yo, k1, k4 (stk-sts). (167 sts)

Rnd 5: In Red Berry, k1, yo, k-tbl of yo, k3, * skp, k4, yo, k1, yo, k4, k2tog *, rep from * to * 11 times more, k4, k-tbl of yo, yo, k1, k4 (stk-sts). (169 sts)

Rnd 6: K1, yo, k-tbl of yo, k all sts, k-tbl of yo, yo, k1, k4 (stk-sts). (171 sts)

Rnd 7: K1, yo, k-tbl of yo, k5, * skp, k3, yo, k3, yo, k3, k2tog *, rep from * to * 11 times more, k6, k-tbl of yo, yo, k1, k4 (stk-sts). (173 sts)

Rnd 8: As Rnd 6. (175 sts)

Rnd 9: K1, yo, k-tbl of yo, k7, * skp, k2, yo, k2tog, yo, k1, yo, skp, yo, k2, k2tog *, rep from * to * 11 times more, k8, k-tbl of yo, yo, k1, 4 stk-sts. (177 sts)

Rnd 10: As Rnd 6. (179 sts)

Rnd 11: K1, yo, k-tbl of yo, k9, * skp, k1, yo, k2tog, yo, k3, yo, skp, yo, k1, k2tog *, rep from * to * 11 times more, k10, k-tbl of yo, yo, k1, k4 (stk-sts). (181 sts)

Rnd 12: As Rnd 6. (183 sts)

Rnd 13: K1, yo, k-tbl of yo, k11, * skp, yo, k2tog, yo, k2tog, yo, k1, yo, skp, yo, skp, yo, k2tog *, rep from * to * 11 times more, k12, yo, k-tbl of yo, k1, k4 (stk-sts). (185 sts)

Rnd 14: As Rnd 6. (187 sts)

Rnds 15–18: In Honey, work as Rnds 1–4. (195 sts)

Rnd 19: In Red Berry, k1, yo, k-tbl of yo, k4, * skp, k4, yo, k1, yo, k4, k2tog *, rep from * to * 13 times more, k5, k-tbl of yo, yo, k1, k4 (stk-sts). (197 sts)

Rnd 20: As Rnd 6. (199 sts)

Rnd 21: K1, yo, k-tbl of yo, k6, * skp, k3, yo, k3, yo, k3, k2tog *, rep from * to * 13 times more, k7, k-tbl of yo, yo, k1, k4 (stk-sts). (201 sts)

Rnd 22: As Rnd 6. (203 sts)

Rnd 23: K1, yo, k-tbl of yo, k8, * skp, k2, yo, k2tog, yo, k1, yo, skp, yo, k2, k2tog *, rep from * to * 13 times more, k9, k-tbl of yo, yo, k1, k4 (stk-sts). (205 sts)

Rnd 24: As Rnd 6. (207 sts)

Rnd 25: K1, yo, k-tbl of yo, k10, * skp, k1, yo, k2tog, yo, k3, yo, skp, yo, k1, k2tog *, rep from * to * 13 times more, k11, k-tbl of yo, yo, k1, k4 (stk-sts). (209 sts)

Rnd 26: As Rnd 6. (211 sts)

Rnd 27: K1, yo, k-tbl of yo, k12, * skp, yo, k2tog, yo, k2tog, yo, k1, yo, skp, yo, skp, yo, k2tog *, rep from * to * 13 times more, k13, k-tbl of yo, yo, k1, k4 (stk-sts). (213 sts)

Rnd 28: As Rnd 6. (215 sts)

Rnds 29–32: In Honey, work as Rnds 1–4. (223 sts)

Rnd 33: In Red Berry, k1, yo, k-tbl of yo, k5, * skp, k4, yo, k1, yo, k4, k2tog *, rep from * to * 15 times more, k6, k-tbl of yo, yo, k1, k4 (stk-sts). (225 sts)

Rnd 34: As Rnd 6. (227 sts)

Rnd 35: K1, yo, k-tbl of yo, k7, * skp, k3, yo, k3, yo, k3, k2tog *, rep from * to * 15 times more, k8, k-tbl of yo, yo, k1, k4 (stk-sts). (229 sts)

Rnd 36: As Rnd 6. (231 sts)

Rnd 37: K1, yo, k-tbl of yo, k9, * skp, k2, yo, k2tog, yo, k1, yo, skp, yo, k2, k2tog *, rep from * to * 15 times more, k10, k-tbl of yo, yo, k1, k4 (stk-sts). (233 sts)

Rnd 38: As Rnd 6. (235 sts)

Rnd 39: K1, yo, k-tbl of yo, k11, * skp, k1, yo, k2tog, yo, k3, yo, skp, yo, k1, k2tog *, rep from * to * 15 times more, k12, k-tbl of yo, yo, k1, k4 (stk-sts). (237 sts)

Rnd 40: As Rnd 6. (239 sts)

Rnd 41: K1, yo, k-tbl of yo, k13, * skp, yo, k2tog, yo, k2tog, yo, k1, yo, skp, yo, skp, yo, k2tog *, rep from * to * 15 times more, k14, k-tbl of yo, k1, k4 (stk-sts). (241 sts)

Rnd 42: As Rnd 6. (243 sts)

Rnds 43–46: In Honey, k1, yo, k-tbl or p-tbl of yo in patt, all sts in garter stitch, k-tbl or p-tbl of yo in patt, yo, k1, k4 (stk-sts). (251 sts)

Rnds 47–48: In Red Berry, k1, yo, k-tbl or p-tbl of yo in patt, all sts in garter stitch, k-tbl or p-tbl of yo in patt, yo, k1, k4 (stk-sts). (255 sts)

Rnds 49–50: In Honey, work as Rnds 47–48. (259 sts)

Rnds 51–52: In Red Berry, work as Rnds 47–48. (263 sts)

Break the working yarn in Red Berry.

BRIOCHE TRIANGLE INSERT

Rnd 1: In Honey, k1, yo, k-tbl of yo, k66, work [(k1, p1) 3 times, k1] in next st, k62, work [(k1, p1) 3 times, k1] in next st, k62, work [(k1, p1) 3 times, k1] in next st, k66, k-tbl of yo, yo, k1, k4 (stk-sts). (277 sts)

Rnd 2: K1, yo, p-tbl of yo, p67, brioche triangle: * brk1, p1 *, rep from * to * 2 times more, brk1, p62, brioche triangle: * brk1, p1 *, rep from * to * 2 times more, brk1, p62, brioche triangle: * knit the brioche sts, p1 *, rep from * to * 2 times more, brk1, p67, p-tbl of yo, yo, k1, k4 (stk-sts). (279 sts)

Rnd 3: K1, yo, k-tbl of yo, k68, brioche triangle: * k1, brp1 *, rep from * to * 2 times more, k1, k62, brioche triangle: * k1, brp1 *, rep from * to * 2 times more, k1, k62, brioche triangle: * k1, brp1 *, rep from * to * 2 times more, k1, k68, k-tbl of yo, yo, k1, k4 (stk-sts). (281 sts)

Rnd 4: Work as Rnd 2. (283 sts)

Rnd 5: Work as Rnd 3. (285 sts)

Rnd 6: Work the rnd as established, at the same time working 5 sts into every first and last brioche st of every triangle as follows: "k1, p1, k1, p1, k1", and incorporate the increased sts into the brioche patt. (311 sts)

Rnds 7–26: Rep Rnds 2–6 another 4 times. (447 sts)

Rnds 27–30: Rep Rnds 2–5 once more (455 sts); then BO the 4 stk-sts.

BORDER

Now, knit a border in zigzag pattern perpendicularly onto the shawl:

CO 8 additional sts into the first st.

Row 1: K7, knit the last stitch together with the next stitch on the left ndl, turn work.

Row 2: K8.

Row 3: K2, yo, k2tog, yo, k2tog, yo, k1, knit the last stitch together with the next stitch on the left ndl, turn work. (9 sts)

Row 4: K9.

Row 5: K2, yo, k2tog, yo, k2tog, yo, k2, knit the last stitch together with the next stitch on the left ndl. (10 sts)

Row 6: K10.

Row 7: K2, yo, k2tog, yo, k2tog, yo, k3, knit the last stitch together with the next stitch on the left ndl. (11 sts)

Row 8: K11.

Row 9: K2, yo, k2tog, yo, k2tog, yo, k4, knit the last stitch together with the next stitch on the left ndl. (12 sts)

Row 10: K12.

Row 11: K2, yo, k2tog, yo, k2tog, yo, k5, knit the last stitch together with the next stitch on the left ndl. (13 sts)

Row 12: K13.

Row 13: BO 5 sts knitwise, k7, knit the last stitch together with the next stitch on the left ndl.

Row 14: K8.

Rep these 14 rows until all sts have been used up, and in the last Row 14, BO all sts loosely.

FINISHING

Now, secure the steek as described in Basics (pp. 16–17); then cut it. Afterward, in Red Berry, p/u sts from the steek edge as follows: * from the next 3 selv sts, p/u 1 st each, skip 1 selv st *, rep from * to the end of the border.

Work 5 rows in stockinette stitch, then BO all sts using elastic BO method (see p. 25), pin the border on the WS, and sew it on. Treat the second steek edge the same way.

Wash the wrap according to the manufacturer's recommendations on the ball band of the yarn, pin it to block, and let it dry. Carefully weave in the remaining ends.

THREE-COLOR SHAWL WITH SLIPPED STITCHES AND GARTER STITCH RIPPLES

Basics

FINISHED SIZE
86.6 x 28.3 in (220 x 72 cm)

TOOLS AND MATERIALS
▸ Rowan Felted Tweed (50% wool, 25% alpaca, 25% Viscose; 191 yd/175 m, 1.75 oz/50 g per skein); 2 skeins #165 Scree, 3 skeins #167 Maritime, and 3 skeins #170 Seafarer
▸ Circular knitting needles, US size 6 (4.0 mm) in different lengths
▸ DPN set, US 6 (4.0 mm)
▸ Stitch markers as needed
▸ Scissors
▸ Tapestry needle for weaving in ends

STITCH PATTERNS
Slipped stitch pattern and ripple pattern: See instructions below.
Slipped stitch (sl1): In RS rows, sl-wyib; in WS rows, sl-wyif; in rnds, sl-wyib.
Garter stitch: In rows: knit on RS and on WS; in rounds, alternate—Rnd 1: knit; Rnd 2: purl.
Steek stitches: Worked as knit sts and not counted in the stitch count.

GAUGE
22 sts and 30 rows = 4 x 4 in (10 x 10 cm)

Instructions

CO 13 sts in Scree.
Rows 1–2: K13.
Row 3: K3, yo, k7, yo, k3. (15 sts)
Row 4: K3, yo, p-tbl of yo, k7, p-tbl of yo, yo, k3. (17 sts)
Row 5: In Maritime k3, yo, k-tbl of yo, k2, sl1, k3, sl1, k2, k-tbl of yo, yo, k3. (19 sts) After this row, CO 9 additional sts for the steek, join to work in the round, and distribute the sts onto a DPN set.
Rnd 6: P3, yo, k-tbl of yo, p3, sl1, p3, sl1, p3, k-tbl of yo, yo, p3, k9 (stk-sts). (21 sts)
Rnd 7: In Scree k3, yo, k-tbl of yo, k13, k-tbl of yo, yo, k3, k9 (stk-sts). (23 sts)
Rnd 8: P3, yo, k-tbl of yo, k15, k-tbl of yo, yo, p3, k9 (stk-sts). (25 sts)
Rnd 9: In Maritime k3, yo, k-tbl of yo, sl1, * k3, sl1 *, rep from * to * 3 times more, k-tbl of yo, yo, k3, k9 (stk-sts). (27 sts)

Rnd 10: P3, yo, p-tbl of yo, p1, sl1, * p3, sl1 *, rep from * to * 3 times more, p1, p-tbl of yo, yo, p3, k9 (stk-sts). (29 sts)
Rnd 11: In Scree k3, yo, k-tbl of yo, k21, k-tbl of yo, yo, k3, k9 (stk-sts). (31 sts)
Rnd 12: P3, yo, k-tbl of yo, k23, k-tbl of yo, yo, p3, k9 (stk-sts). (33 sts)
Rnd 13: In Maritime k3, yo, k-tbl of yo, k2, 1 slipped stitch, * k3, sl1 *, rep from * to * 4 times more, k2, k-tbl of yo, yo, k3, k9 (stk-sts). (35 sts)
Rnd 14: P3, yo, p-tbl of yo, * p3, sl1 *, rep from * to * 5 times more, p3, p-tbl of yo, yo, p3, k9 (stk-sts). (37 sts)
Rnd 15: In Scree k3, yo, k-tbl of yo, k29, k-tbl of yo, yo, k3, k9 (stk-sts). (39 sts)
Rnd 16: P3, yo, k-tbl of yo, k31, k-tbl of yo, yo, p3, k9 (stk-sts). (41 sts)
Rnds 17–96: Work Rnds 13–16 another 20 times. (201 sts)

IN SCREE, WORK RIPPLE PATTERN

Rnds 1–2: 3 sts garter stitch, yo, k-tbl of yo, Rnd 1: k193 (Rnd 2: k195), k-tbl of yo, yo, 3 sts garter stitch, k9 (stk-sts). (205 sts)

Rnd 3: K3, yo, k-tbl of yo, k4, * k1, yo, k1, 2 yo's, k1, 3 yo's, k1, 2 yo's, k1, yo, k4 *, rep from * to * 20 times more, k4, k-tbl of yo, yo, k3, k9 (stk-sts). (207 sts, not counting the yo's of the ripple patt)

Rnd 4: 3 sts garter stitch, yo, p-tbl of yo, p199, dropping all yo's, p-tbl of yo, yo, 3 sts garter stitch, k9 (stk-sts). (209 sts)

Rnds 5–6: 3 sts garter stitch, yo, either k-tbl or p-tbl of yo in patt, Rnd 5: 201 sts garter stitch (Rnd 6: 203), k-tbl or p-tbl of yo in patt, yo, 3 sts garter stitch, k9 (stk-sts). (213 sts)

Rnd 7: K3, yo, k-tbl of yo, k8, * k5, yo, k1, 2 yo's, k1, 3 yo's, k1, 2 yo's, k1, yo *, rep from * to * 20 times more, 8 sts garter stitch, k-tbl of yo, yo, k3, k9 (stk-sts). (215 sts, not counting the yo's of the ripple patt)

Rnd 8: Work as Rnd 4. (217 sts)

Rnds 9–10: Work as Rnds 5–6. (221 sts)

Rnd 11: K3, yo, k-tbl of yo, k3, * k1, yo, k1, 2 yo's, k1, 3 yo's, k1, 2 yo's, k1, yo, k4 *, rep from * to * 22 times more, k3, k-tbl of yo, yo, 3 sts garter stitch, k9 (stk-sts). (223 sts, not counting the yo's of the ripple patt)

Rnd 12: Work as Rnd 4. (225 sts)

Rnds 13–14: Work as Rnds 5–6. (229 sts)

CONTINUE IN SLIPPED-STITCH PATTERN

Rnds 1–2: In Maritime, 3 sts garter stitch, yo, k-tbl or p-tbl of yo in patt, Rnd 1: 221 sts (Rnd 2: 223 sts) in stockinette stitch, k-tbl or p-tbl of yo in patt, yo, 3 sts garter stitch, k9 (stk-sts). (233 sts)

Rnds 3–4: In Scree, 3 sts garter stitch, yo, k-tbl or p-tbl of yo in patt, (Rnd 4: p1), * sl1, 3 sts garter stitch *, rep from * to * 55 times more, sl1, (Rnd 4: p1), k-tbl or p-tbl of yo in patt, yo, 3 sts garter stitch, k9 (stk-sts). (237 sts)

Rnds 5–40: Rep Rnds 1–4 another 9 times, always working 2 more patt repeats of the slipped stitch patt every time. (309 sts)

Rnds 41–42: Work as Rnds 1–2 (313 sts); then break the working yarn in Scree.

IN MARITIME, WORK IN RIPPLE PATTERN

Rnds 1–2: 3 sts garter stitch, yo, k-tbl or p-tbl of yo in patt, Rnd 1: k305 (Rnd 2: k307), k-tbl or p-tbl of yo in patt, yo, 3 sts garter stitch, k9 (stk-sts). (317 sts)

Rnd 3: K3, yo, k-tbl of yo, k3, * k1, yo, k1, yo 2 times, k1, yo 3 times, k1, yo 2 times, k1, yo, k4 *, rep from * to * 33 times more, k-tbl of yo, yo, k3, k9 (stk-sts). (319 sts, not counting the yo's of the ripple pattern)

Rnd 4: P3, yo, p-tbl of yo, p311, dropping all yo's, p-tbl of yo, yo, p3, k9 (stk-sts). (321 sts)

Rnds 5–6: 3 sts garter stitch, yo, k-tbl or p-tbl of yo in patt, 313 sts garter stitch, k-tbl or p-tbl of yo in patt, yo, 3 sts garter stitch, k9 (stk-sts). (325 sts)

Rnd 7: K3, yo, k-tbl of yo, k7, * k5, yo, k1, yo 2 times, k1, yo 3 times, k1, yo 2 times, k1, yo *, rep from * to * 33 times more, k4, k-tbl of yo, yo, k3, k9 (stk-sts). (327 sts, not counting the yo's of the ripple pattern)

Rnd 8: Work as Rnd 4. (329 sts)

Rnds 9–10: Work as Rnds 5–6. (333 sts)

Rnd 11: K3, yo, k-tbl of yo, k2, * k1, yo, k1, yo 2 times, k1, yo 3 times, k1, yo 2 times, k1, yo, k4 *, rep from * to * 34 times more, k8, k-tbl of yo, yo, k3, k9 (stk-sts). (335 sts)

Rnd 12: Work as Rnd 4. (337 sts)

Rnds 13–14: Work as Rnds 5–6. (341 sts)

CONTINUE IN SLIPPED-STITCH PATTERN

Rnds 1–2: In Maritime, 3 sts garter stitch, yo, k-tbl or p-tbl of yo in patt, Rnd 1: 333 sts (Rnd 2: 335 sts) in stockinette stitch, k-tbl or p-tbl of yo in patt, yo, 3 sts garter stitch, k9 (stk-sts). (345 sts)

Rnds 3–4: In Seafarer, 3 sts garter stitch, yo, k-tbl or p-tbl of yo in patt, (Rnd 4: k1), * sl1, 3 sts garter stitch *, rep from * to * 83 times more, sl1, (Rnd 4: k1), k-tbl or p-tbl of yo in patt, yo, 3 sts garter stitch, k9 (stk-sts). (349 sts)

Rnds 5–40: Rep Rnds 1–4 another 9 times, always working 2 more patt reps every time. (421 sts)

Rnds 41–42: Rep Rnds 1–2 once more (425 sts). Break the working yarn in Maritime.

IN SEAFARER, WORK IN RIPPLE PATTERN

Rnds 1–2: 3 sts garter stitch, yo, k-tbl or p-tbl of yo in patt, Rnd 1: k417 (Rnd 2: k419), k-tbl or p-tbl of yo in patt, yo, 3 sts garter stitch, k9 (stk-sts). (429 sts)

Rnd 3: K3, yo, k-tbl of yo, k5, * k1, yo, k1, yo 2 times, k1, yo 3 times, k1, yo 2 times, k1, yo, k4 *, rep from * to * 45 times more, k2, k-tbl of yo, yo, k3, k9 (stk-sts). (431 sts, not counting the yo's of the ripple patt)

Rnd 4: P3, yo, p-tbl of yo, 423 sts garter stitch, dropping all yo's, p-tbl of yo, yo, p3, k9 (stk-sts). (433 sts)

Rnds 5–6: 3 sts garter stitch, yo, k-tbl or p-tbl of yo in patt, Rnd 5: 425 sts (Rnd 6: 427 sts) garter stitch, k-tbl or p-tbl of yo in patt, yo, 3 sts garter stitch, k9 (stk-sts). (437 sts)

Rnd 7: K3, yo, k-tbl of yo, k9, * k5, yo, k1, yo 2 times, k1, yo 3 times, k1, yo 2 times, k1, yo *, rep from * to * 45 times more, k6, k-tbl of yo, yo, k3, k9 (stk-sts). (439 sts, not counting the yo's of the ripple patt)

Rnd 8: Work as Rnd 4. (441 sts)

Rnds 9–10: Work as Rnds 5–6. (445 sts)

Rnd 11: K3, yo, k-tbl or p-tbl of yo in patt, k3, * k1, yo, k1, yo 2 times, k1, yo 3 times, k1, yo 2 times, k1, yo, k4 *, rep from * to * 47 times more, k2, k-tbl of yo, yo, 3 sts garter stitch, k9 (stk-sts). (447 sts)

Rnd 12: Work as Rnd 4. (449 sts)

Rnds 13–14: Work as Rnds 5–6. (451 sts) In the last rnd, BO the steek sts and then knit 1 row more. BO all sts loosely on the WS.

FINISHING

Secure the steek as described in Basics (pp. 16–17); then cut it.

Fold over the stk-sts to the WS twice, pin, and sew on.

Wash the wrap according to the manufacturer's recommendations on the ball band of the yarn, pin it to block, and let it dry. Weave in all remaining ends.

Kari
PATTERN MIX STOLE

Basics

FINISHED SIZE
69 x 21.65 in (175 x 55 cm)

TOOLS AND MATERIALS
▸ Lang Yarns Gordon (92% wool, 8% cashmere; 208 yd/190 m, 1.75 oz/50 g per skein); 6 skeins #0065 Azalea
▸ Circular knitting needle, US size 6 (4.0 mm), 32 in (80 cm) long
▸ Spare circular needle, US size 4 (3.5 mm)
▸ Cable or auxiliary needle
▸ Stitch markers as needed
▸ Scissors
▸ Tapestry needle for weaving in ends

STITCH PATTERNS
Selvedge stitches: In rows: In RS rows, slip the first st, and knit the last st; in WS rows, slip the first st, and purl the last st. In rnds: knit all selv sts in all rounds.
Steek stitches: Worked in stockinette st and not counted in the stitch count.
Stockinette stitch: In rows: knit on RS, purl on WS; in rounds: knit all sts in all rounds.
Lace and cable patterns: See written instructions and chart. In the chart, all rounds are shown. Read the chart from right to left. Due to limited space on the page, the knitting chart is divided into a left and right half. In every round, first the sts of Chart 1 are worked right to left, then 16 center sts are worked (knit in odd-numbered rounds, purl in even-numbered rounds), and then the sts of Chart 2 are

worked right to left. Stitches shown in the knitting chart are enclosed in parentheses in the written instructions.
Please note: *Cable stitches shown in the chart as knit sts are to be knitted through the back loop. Outside of the cables, there are separate symbols for regular knit sts and those knit through the back loop.*

GAUGE
In stockinette stitch on US 6 (4.0 mm) needles:
20 sts and 31 rows = 4 x 4 in (10 x 10 cm)

Instructions

CO 110 sts, and work zigzag edging as follows:
Rows 1–6: Selv st, 108 sts in stockinette stitch, k the selv st.
Row 7: Selv st, * skp, yo *, rep from * to * 53 times more, selv st.
Row 8: Selv st, p108, selv st.
Rows 9–14: Selv st, 108 sts in stockinette stitch, selv st.
Now, using a spare circular in size US 4 (3.5 mm), insert needle between every stitch leg of the CO row sts, and let the sts slide onto the needle. Hold the spare needle with the picked-up sts parallel behind the main needle, and knit the sts from both needles together in pairs: always 1 st from the front needle with 1 st

from the back needle.
CO an additional 9 sts for the steek, and join to work in the round. If preferred, placing markers before and after the steek sts is helpful.
Rnd 1: (Chart #1: selv st, k3, * skp, yo *, rep from * to * 5 times more, p3, * k1-tbl, p1 *, rep from * to * 5 times more, k1-tbl, p3, * skp, yo *, rep from * to * 5 times more), k16, (Chart #2: * yo, skp *, rep from * to * 5 times more, p3, * k1-tbl, p1 *, rep from * to * 5 times more, k1-tbl, p3, * yo, skp *, rep from * to * 5 times more, k3, selv st), k9 (stk-sts).
Rnd 2: (Chart #1: selv st, k15, p3, * k1-tbl, p1 *, rep from * to * 5 times more, k1-tbl, p3, k12), p16, (Chart #2: k12, p3, * k1-tbl, p1 *, rep from * to * 5 times more, k1-tbl, p3, k15, selv st), k9 (stk-sts).
Rnds 3–8: Rep Rnds 1–2 another 3 times.
Rnd 9: (Chart #1: selv st, k3, * skp, yo *, rep from * to * 5 times more, p3, hold 6 sts on cable needle behind work, * k1-tbl, p1 *, rep from * to * 2 times more, k1-tbl, then work the sts from the cable needle as (p1, k1-tbl) 3 times; p3, * skp, yo *, rep from * to * 5 times more), k16, (Chart #2: * yo, skp *, rep from * to * 5 times more, p3, hold 6 sts on cable needle behind work, * k1-tbl, p1 *, rep from * to * 2 times more, k1-tbl, then work the sts from the cable needle as (p1, k1-tbl) 3 times; p3, * yo, skp *, rep from * to * 5 times more, k3, selv st), k9 (stk-sts).

Rnd 10: Work as Rnd 2.

Rnds 11–12: Work as Rnds 1–2.

Rep these 12 rnds a total of 32 times (= 384 rnds); then in the last rnd, BO the 9 stk-sts knitwise, and continue, working a zigzag border in back-and-forth rows:

Rows 1–6: Selv st, 108 sts in stockinette stitch, selv st.

Row 7: Selv st, * skp, yo *, rep from * to * 53 times more, selv st.

Row 8: Selv st, p108, selv st.

Rows 9–14: Selv st, 108 sts in stockinette stitch, selv st.

Now, using a spare circular in size US 4 (3.5 mm), insert the needle into every stitch in the first row of stockinette from the back of the work, and let the sts slide onto the spare needle. Hold the spare needle with the picked-up sts parallel behind the main needle, and BO all sts knitwise with 3 needles: always knit 1 st from the front needle together with 1 st from the back needle, while binding off knitwise at the same time.

FINISHING

Secure the steek as described in Basics (pp. 16–17); then cut it. Fold over the stk-sts to the WS twice, pin, and sew on.
Wash the stole according to the manufacturer's recommendations on the ball band of the yarn, pin it to block, and let it dry. Carefully weave in the remaining ends.

CHART #1

Refer to key on p. 26.

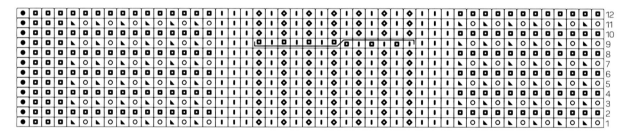

CHART #2

Owing to space constraints, the knitting chart had to be divided into two parts for the book. In every round: first, the 46 sts of Chart #1 are worked from right to left, then the 16 center sts are worked (knit in odd-numbered rounds, purl in even-numbered rounds), and then the 46 sts of Chart #2 are worked from right to left.

Please note: **Within cables,** those cable stitches shown in the chart as "knit" are to be knitted **through the back loop.** Outside of the cables, there are separate symbols for regular knit sts and those knit through the back loop.

Ebba

DELICATE LACE STOLE

Basics

FINISHED SIZE
78.8 x 15.7 in (200 x 40 cm)

TOOLS AND MATERIALS
▶ Ito Yarn Karei (100% cashmere; 191 yd/175 m, 0.9 oz/25 g per skein); 5 skeins #804 OrientBlue
▶ Circular knitting needle, US size 4 (3.5 mm), 24 in (60 cm) long
▶ 7 stitch markers
▶ Scissors
▶ Tapestry needle for weaving in ends

PATTERN NOTES
▶ The shawl is worked from the bottom up, starting at the tip. The special elongated shape with a flat tip is achieved by short row shaping.
▶ For better orientation, place stitch markers before and after the 4 selv sts, between pattern repeats, and before and after the steek sts.

GAUGE
In stockinette stitch on US 4 (3.5 mm) needles:
27 sts and 22 rows = 4 x 4 in (10 x 10 cm)

STITCH PATTERNS
Selvedge stitches: In rows: slip the first st, knit the last st.
Garter stitch: In rows: knit all sts in all rows; in rounds, alternate—Rnd 1: knit; Rnd 2: purl.
Lace pattern: See written instructions and chart. In the chart, all rounds are shown. Read the chart from right to left. The marked patt repeat is worked 4 times around in every round.
Steek stitches: Worked as knit sts and not counted in the stitch count.

Instructions

CO 88 sts.
Work 10 rows in garter stitch; in the last row, CO 9 additional sts for the steek, and join to work in the round.
Rnd 1: K4, * ssk, k8, yo 9 times, k8, k2tog *, rep from * to * 3 times more, k4, k9 (stk-sts). (116 sts)
Rnd 2: P4, * ssk, k7, k9-tbl, k7, k2tog *, rep from * to * 3 times more, p4, k9 (stk-sts). (108 sts)
Rnd 3: K4, * ssk, k21, k2tog *, rep from * to * 3 times more, k4, k9 (stk-sts). (100 sts)
Rnd 4: P4, * ssk, k19, k2tog *, rep from * to * 3 times more, p4, k9 (stk-sts). (92 sts)
Rnd 5: K4, * ssk, k17, k2tog *, rep from * to * 3 times more, k4, k9 (stk-sts). (84 sts)

Rnd 6: P4, * ssk, k3, yo 4 times, k3, yo 4 times, k3, yo 4 times, k3, yo 4 times, k3, k2tog *, rep from * to * 3 times more, p4, k9 (stk-sts). (140 sts)
Rnd 7: K4, * ssk, k2, k4-tbl, k3, k4-tbl, k3, k4-tbl, k3, k4-tbl, k2, k2tog *, rep from * to * 3 times more, k4, k9 (stk-sts). (132 sts)
Rnd 8: P4, * ssk, k27, k2tog *, rep from * to * 3 times more, p4, k9 (stk-sts). (124 sts)
Rnd 9: K4, * ssk, k25, k2tog *, rep from * to * 3 times more, k4, k9 (stk-sts). (116 sts)
Rnd 10: P4, * ssk, k1, yo, (k2tog, yo) 11 times, k2tog *, rep from * to * 3 times more, p4, k9 (stk-sts). (112 sts)
Rnd 11: K4, * ssk, k22, k2tog *, rep from * to * 3 times more, k4, k9 (stk-sts). (104 sts)
Rnd 12: P4, * ssk, k20, k2tog *, rep from * to * 3 times more, p4, k9 (stk-sts). (96 sts)
Rnd 13: K4, * ssk, k18, k2tog *, rep from * to * 3 times more, k4, k9 (stk-sts). (88 sts)
Rnd 14: P4, * p20 *, rep from * to * 3 times more, p4, k9 (stk-sts).
Rnd 15: Work as Rnd 14.
Work these 15 rnds a total of 34 times; in the last rnd, BO the 9 stk-sts knitwise and continue in turned rows.
Work 10 rows in garter stitch; then BO all sts, using elastic BO method (see p. 25).

FINISHING

Now, secure the steek as described in Basics (pp. 16–17); then cut it.

Fold over the stk-sts to the WS twice, pin, and sew on.

Wash the stole according to the manufacturer's recommendations on the ball band of the yarn, skillfully pin it to block, and let it dry. Carefully weave in the remaining ends.

Refer to key on p. 26.

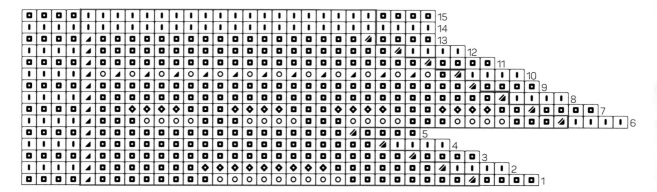

Work the pattern repeat (marked in red)
4 times around in every round.

Nora

TRIANGULAR SHAWL WITH SLIPPED STITCH PATTERN AND FEATHER-AND-FAN BORDER

Basics

FINISHED SIZE
86.6 x 27.6 in (220 x 70 cm)

TOOLS AND MATERIALS
▸ Amano Yarns Puna (100% baby alpaca; 273 yd/250 m, 3.5 oz/100 g per skein); 2 skeins #4008 Santa Catalina and 2 skeins #4000 Maras White
▸ Circular knitting needles, US size 6 (4.0 mm) in different lengths
▸ DPN set, US size 6 (4.0 mm)
▸ Stitch markers as needed
▸ Scissors
▸ Tapestry needle for weaving in ends

STITCH PATTERNS
Slipped stitch pattern: See knitting chart and additional explanations in written instructions; shown are the first 3 rows/rounds as well as a chart for the main pattern. The pattern is worked alternating 2 rows/rounds in Maras White and 2 rows/rounds in Santa Catalina.

Feather-and-fan pattern border: Chart shows a patt rep in width and height and the stitches before and after the rep.

Stitches slipped knitwise (sl1-k): Slip 1 st with yarn in back of work.

Stitches slipped purlwise (sl1-p): Slip 1 st with yarn in front of work.

Stockinette stitch: In rows: knit on RS, purl on WS; in rounds: knit all sts in all rounds.

Selvedge stitches: In rows: knit on RS, purl on WS; in rounds: knit all selv sts in all rounds.

Steek stitches: Worked as knit sts and not counted in the stitch count.

GAUGE
In stockinette stitch on US 6 (4.0 mm) needles:
22 sts and 28 rows = 4 x 4 in (10 x 10 cm)

Instructions

CO 5 sts in Maras White.
Work 2 rows in stockinette stitch and then continue from chart.

Row 1: In Santa Catalina, k1, sl1-k, k1, sl1-k, k1. (5 sts)

Row 2: P1, M1-p, sl1-p, p1, sl1-p, M1-p, p1. (7 sts)

Row 3: In Maras White, k1, M1-k, sl1-k, k1, sl1-k, k1, sl1-k, M1-k, k1. (9 sts)

Row 4: P1, M1-p, * p1, sl1-p *, rep from * to * 2 times more, p1, M1-p, p1. (11 sts)

Row 5: In Santa Catalina, k1, M1-k, * k1, sl1-k *, rep from * to * 3 times more, k1, M1-k, k1. (13 sts)

After this row, CO 9 additional sts for the steek, and join into the round.

Rnd 6: Selv st, M1-k, * sl1-k, k1 *, rep from * to * 4 times more, k1, M1-k, selv st, k9 (stk-sts). (15 sts)

Rnds 7–34: Continue from chart, always alternating 2 rnds in Maras White and 2 rnds in Santa Catalina. (71 sts)

Rnd 35: Selv st, M1-k, work sts #6–24 of Row 7 of Chart #2 once, then work sts #1–24 twice (full pattern repeat), then work sts #1 and 2 of Row 7 of Chart #2 once, M1-k, selv st, k9 (stk-sts). (73 sts)

Rnds 36–230: Continue the pattern according to Chart #2; increases are worked from the bar between sts in every round after the first and before the last selv st. Incorporate sts increased at the beginning of the round to the right of the patt repeat in the chart, sts increased at the end of the round always to the left of the patt repeat in the chart, and work additional full patt reps as soon as enough sts for a full rep have accumulated. Work the patt rep 8 times total, heightwise. (453 sts)

Rnds 231–232: Knit 2 rnds in Maras White. (457 sts)

BORDER

Now, continue with feather-and-fan pattern border in Maras White from Chart #3:
Rnd 1: Selv st, M1-k, k3, * (k2tog) 3 times, (yo, k1) 6 times, (k2tog) 3 times *, rep from * to * 24 times more, k2, M1-k, selv st, k9 (stk-sts). (459 sts)

Rnds 2–3: Selv st, M1-k, k to selv st, M1-k, selv st, k9 (stk-sts).
Rep Rnds 1–3 another 5 times, knitting sts increased before and after the selv st. In the last rnd, BO the steek sts. Then, BO all sts with applied i-cord (see p. 23).

FINISHING

Secure the steek as described in Basics (pp. 16–17); then cut it.
Fold over the stk-sts to the WS twice, pin, and sew on.
Wash the shawl according to the manufacturer's recommendations on the ball band of the yarn, skillfully pin it to block, and let it dry.
Carefully weave in the remaining ends.

CHART #1

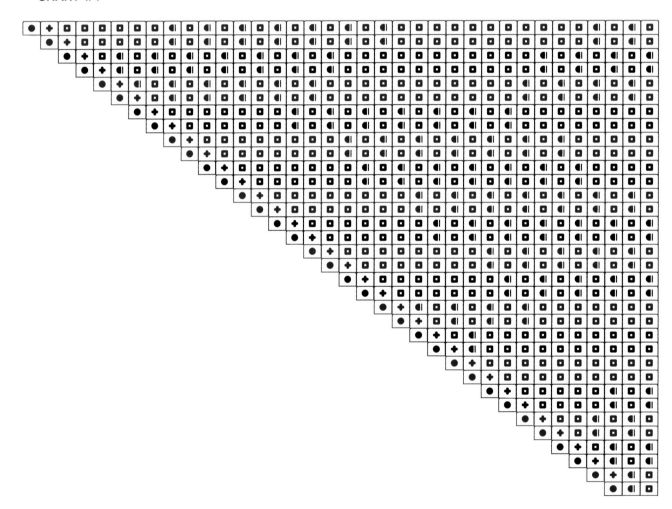

Refer to key on p. 26.

CHART #2: PATTERN REPEAT

Refer to key on p. 26.

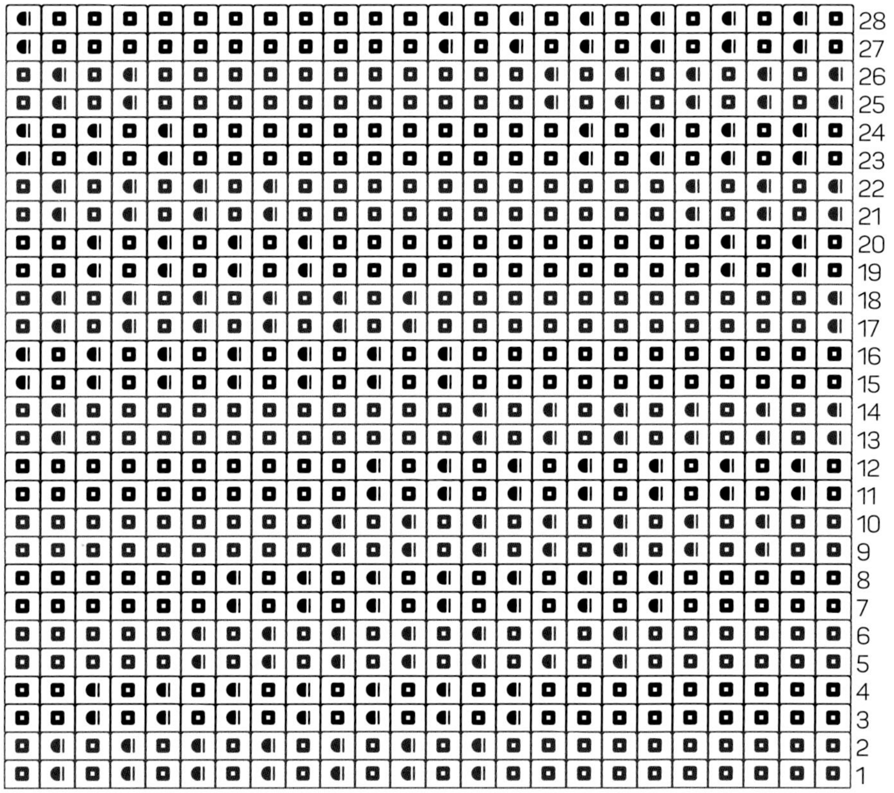

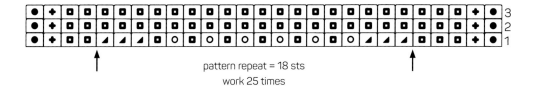

CHART #3: FEATHER-AND-FAN PATTERN BORDER

Refer to key on p. 26.

pattern repeat = 18 sts
work 25 times

Tuva

STOLE IN JAPANESE STITCH

Basics

FINISHED SIZE
67 x 17.7 in (170 x 45 cm)

MATERIAL
- Rowan Moordale (70% wool, 30% alpaca; 251 yd/230 m, 3.5 oz/100 g per skein); 3 skeins #003 Turmeric
- Circular knitting needles, US size 6 (4.0 mm), 24 and 48–60 in (60 cm and 120–150 cm) long
- Stitch markers as needed
- Scissors
- Tapestry needle for weaving in ends

STITCH PATTERNS
Japanese stitch: See written instructions and chart. All patt rounds are shown in the chart; the chart shows the first 4 sts, the stitch patt rep of the main patt (18 sts wide), and the last stitch. The patt rep is worked 3 times around. The chart is to be read from right to left.
Border: Alternate k1-tbl, p1.
Selvedge stitches: Knit.
Steek stitches: Worked as knit sts and not counted in the stitch count.

GAUGE
In stockinette stitch on US 6 (4.0 mm) needles:
23 sts and 30 rows = 4 x 4 in (10 x 10 cm)

Instructions

CO 68 sts and join into the round, dividing sts as follows: Selv st, k57 for the stitch pattern, selv st, k9 (stk-sts).
Setup Rnd: Selv st, p3, * (k1, p1) 4 times, k7, p3 *, rep from * to * 2 times more, selv st, 9 stk-sts. From here on, work from chart.
Rnd 1: Selv st, p3, * (k1-tbl, p1) 4 times, sssk, yo, k1, yo, sk2p, p3 *, rep from * to * 2 times more, selv st, k9 (stk-sts).
Rnd 2: Selv st, p3, * (k1-tbl, p1) 4 times, k1, yo, k3, yo, k1, p3 *, rep from * to * 2 times more, selv st, k9 (stk-sts).
Rnds 3–4: Selv st, p3, * (k1-tbl, p1) 4 times, k7, p3 *, rep from * to * 2 times more, selv st, k9 (stk-sts).
Rnds 5–16: Work Rnds 1–4 another 3 times.
Rnd 17: Selv st, p3, * sssk, yo, k1, yo, sk2p, (p1, k1-tbl) 4 times, p3 *, rep from * to * 2 times more, selv st, k9 (stk-sts).
Rnd 18: Selv st, p3, * k1, yo, k3, yo, k1, (p1, k1-tbl) 4 times, p3 *, rep from * to * 2 times more, selv st, k9 (stk-sts).
Rnds 19–20: Selv st, p3, * k7, (p1, k1-tbl) 4 times, p3 *, rep from * to * 2 times more, selv st, k9 (stk-sts).
Rnds 21–32: Work Rnds 17–20 another 3 times.

Work these 32 rnds a total of 13 times height-wise; then BO sts loosely.
Now, secure the steek as described in Basics (pp. 16–17); then cut it. Fold over the stk-sts to the WS twice, pin, and sew on.

BORDER
For the border, p/u and k sts directly from the selv sts as follows: Along the long edges, 213 sts each, along the short edges, 39 sts each, and at each corner, 1 st. (508 sts)
Rnd 1: Starting at the long edge: k1-tbl, * p1, k1-tbl *, rep from * to * to next corner stitch, k1 (= corner stitch), k1-tbl, * p1, k1-tbl *, rep from * to * to next corner stitch, k1 (= corner stitch), k1-tbl, * p1, k1-tbl *, rep from * to * to next corner stitch, k1 (= corner stitch), k1-tbl, * p1, k1-tbl *, rep from * to * to next corner stitch, k1 (= corner stitch).
Rep this rnd another 12 times, at the same time increasing 1 st each from the bar between sts in pattern (either M1-k, or M1-p) before and after every corner stitch in Rnds 2, 5, 8, and 11.
Rnd 14: Yo, p1, * yo, skp *, rep from * to * to next corner stitch, yo, k1 (= corner stitch), yo, p1, * 1 yo, skp *, rep from * to * to next corner stitch, yo, k1 (= corner stitch), yo, p1, * yo, skp *, rep from * to * to next corner stitch, yo, k1 (= corner stitch), yo, p1, * 1 yo, skp *, rep from * to * to next corner stitch, yo, k1 (= corner stitch).
Rnd 15: * Yo, skp *, rep from * to * to next corner stitch, yo, k1 (= corner stitch), * yo,

skp *, rep from * to * to next corner stitch, yo, k1 (= corner stitch), * yo, skp *, rep from * to * to next corner stitch, yo, k1 (= corner stitch), * yo, skp *, rep from * to * to next corner stitch, yo, k1 (= corner stitch).

Rnd 16: * P1, k1-tbl *, rep from * to * to next corner stitch, p1, k1 (= corner stitch), work the remaining 3 sides in the same manner.

Rnd 17: Work as Rnd 16.

Rnd 18: * Yo, skp *, rep from * to * to next corner stitch, yo, k1 (= corner stitch), work the remaining 3 sides in the same manner.

Rnd 19: Work all sts as they appear; then BO all sts, using elastic BO method (see p. 25).

FINISHING

Wash the stole according to the manufacturer's recommendations on the ball band of the yarn, pin it to block, and let it dry. Carefully weave in the remaining ends.

KNITTING CHART

Refer to key on p. 26.

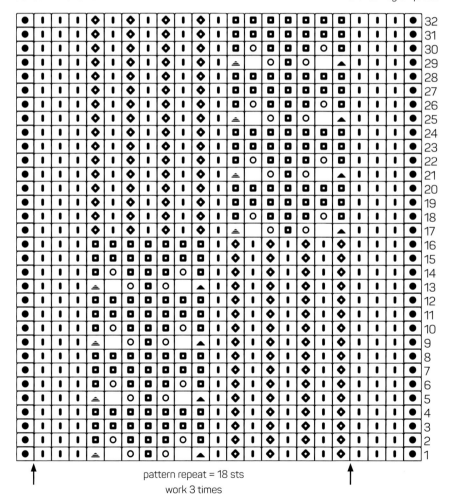

pattern repeat = 18 sts
work 3 times

TRIANGULAR SHAWL WITH BRIOCHE PATTERN AND MINI CABLES

Basics

FINISHED SIZE
63 x 29.1 in (160 x 74 cm)

TOOLS AND MATERIALS
▶ Rowan Moordale (70% wool, 30% alpaca; 251 yd/230 m, 3.5 oz/100 g per skein); 3 skeins #008 Blue Moor
▶ Circular knitting needles, US size 6 (4.0 mm) in different lengths
▶ DPN set, US size 6 (4.0 mm)
▶ Cable or auxiliary needle
▶ Stitch markers as needed
▶ Scissors
▶ Tapestry needle for weaving in ends

STITCH PATTERNS
Main pattern: Alternate 1 brioche st, 5 sts garter stitch.

Garter stitch: In rows: knit all sts in all rows; in rounds, alternate—Rnd 1: knit; Rnd 2: purl.

Brioche knit (brk): Rnd 1: k1, Rnd 2: insert the right needle from front to back into the stitch 1 rnd below the st to be worked, pull the working yarn through this st, and lift it onto the right needle. This dissolves the st above and places it like a yarn over, onto the needle.

Cable: Work as stated in instructions, i.e., before the center sts: hold 3 sts on cable needle behind work, k3 and then k3 from cable needle; after the center sts: hold 3 sts on cable needle in front of work, k3 and then k3 from cable needle.

Selvedge stitches: Work the first 3 sts and the last 3 sts of every row or round always in garter stitch.

Steek stitches: Worked as knit sts and not counted in the stitch count.

GAUGE
In stockinette stitch on US 6 (4.0 mm) needles:
23 sts and 30 rows = 4 x 4 in (10 x 10 cm)

Instructions

CO 4 sts.
Row 1: K1, yo, k2 (= ctr-sts), yo, k1. (6 sts)
Row 2: P1, yo, k-tbl of yo, p2 (= ctr-sts), k-tbl of yo, yo, p1. (8 sts)
Row 3: K1, yo, k-tbl of yo, k1, M1-k, k2 (= ctr-sts), M1-k, k1, k-tbl of yo, yo, k1. (12 sts)
Row 4: P1, yo, k-tbl of yo, k3, p2 (= ctr-sts), k3, k-tbl of yo, yo, p1. (14 sts)
Row 5: K3, M1-k, k3, M1-k, k2 (= ctr-sts), M1-k, k3, M1-k, k3. (18 sts)
Row 6: P1, k7, p2 (= ctr-sts), k7, p1.
Row 7: K3, M1-k, k5, M1-k, k2 (= ctr-sts), M1-k, k5, M1-k, k3. (22 sts)
Row 8: P4, k5, p1, p2 (= ctr-sts), p1, k5, p4.
After this row, CO 4 additional sts for the steek, distribute all sts onto a DPN set, and join into the round.
Rnd 1 (Work brioche sts 1 row below): K3, M1-k, brk1, k5, brk1, M1-k, k2 (= ctr-sts), M1-k, brk1, k5, brk1, M1-k, k3, k4 (stk-sts). (26 sts)

Rnd 2 (Knit the brioche sts): P4, knit the brioche sts, p5, brk1, p1, k2 (= ctr-sts), p1, brk1, p5, brk1, p4, k4 (stk-sts).
Rnds 3–34: Rep Rnds 1–2 another 16 times, incorporating the increased sts into the main patt (brk1, 5 sts garter stitch). (90 sts)
After having completed the last round, the following sts are on the needles: 3 knit sts, (5 sts garter stitch, brk1) 6 times, 5 sts garter stitch, 2 knit sts (= ctr-sts), 5 sts garter stitch, (brk1, 5 sts garter stitch) 6 times, 3 knit sts, 4 stk-sts. (90 sts)
Rnd 35: K3, M1-k, * 5 sts garter stitch, brk1 *, rep from * to * 5 times more, 5 sts garter stitch, M1-k, k2 (= ctr-sts), M1-k, 5 sts garter stitch, * brk1, 5 sts garter stitch*, rep from * to * 5 times more, M1-k, k3, k4 (stk-sts). (94 sts)
Rnd 36: Work all sts in pattern, only the increases before and after the 2 center sts are worked in stockinette stitch.
Rnds 37–46: Work Rnds 35–36 another 5 times. (114 sts)
Rnd 47: K3, M1-k, * 5 sts garter stitch, brk1 *, rep from * to * 6 times more, 5 sts garter stitch, hold 3 sts on cable needle behind work, k3, then k3 from cable needle, k2 (= ctr-sts), hold 3 sts on cable needle in front of work, k3, then k3 from cable needle, 5 sts garter stitch, * brk1, 5 sts garter stitch *, rep from * to * 6 times more, M1-k, k3, k4 (stk-sts). (116 sts)
Rnd 48: Work all sts in patt, incorporating the increased sts into the main patt; the sts of the 6 sts wide cable are continued as established, and are cabled in every 12th round.

Rnd 49: K3, M1-k, * 5 sts garter stitch, brk1 *, rep from * to * to directly before the 2 ctr sts, M1-k, k2 (= ctr-sts), M1-k, * brk1, 5 sts garter stitch*, rep from * to * to 3 sts before the stk-sts, M1-k, k3, k4 (stk-sts). (120 sts)

Rnd 50: Work all sts in pattern.

Rows 51–88: Work Rnds 49–50 another 19 times. (196 sts)

Rows 89–102: Rep only Rnds 35–48 once more. (222 sts)

Rows 103–142: Work Rnds 49–50 another 20 times. (302 sts)

Rows 143–156: Rep only Rnds 35–48 once more. (328 sts)

Rows 157–188: Work Rnds 49–50 another 16 times (392 sts); then BO all sts loosely.

FINISHING

Secure the steek as described in Basics (pp. 16–17); then cut it.

P/u and knit sts from the first stitch after the stk-sts as follows: * from the next 3 sts, p/u 1 st each, skip 1 st *, rep from * to * to the end of the steek edge.

Afterward, work 5 rows more in stockinette stitch, and BO sts using elastic BO method (see p. 25). Fold this small facing to the wrong side, pin it in place, and sew it on.

Treat the second steek edge the same way.

Wash the wrap according to the manufacturer's recommendations on the ball band of the yarn, pin it to block, and let it dry. Carefully weave in the remaining ends.

DELICATE LACE STOLE

Basics

FINISHED SIZE
63 x 19.7 in (160 x 50 cm)

TOOLS AND MATERIALS
- Ito Yarn Rakuda (70% wool, 30% camel hair; 231 yd/212 m, 1.4 oz/40 g per skein); 4 skeins #653 Pale Blush and 2 skeins #654 White
- Circular knitting needle, US size 4 (3.5 mm), 24 in (60 cm) and 48–60 in (120–150 cm) or longer
- Cable or auxiliary needle
- Stitch markers as needed
- Scissors
- Tapestry needle for weaving in ends

STITCH PATTERNS
Selvedge stitches: Knit.

Lace pattern: See written instructions and chart. The chart shows the first 8 sts, the framed patt rep, which is worked 6 times around in every round, and the last 8 sts.

Please note: *Rnd 27 is divided into repeats differently since the pattern repeat needs a different stitch count in this round. Please refer to the written instructions here as well. The chart is to be read from right to left.*

Steek stitches: Worked as knit sts and not counted in the stitch count.

GAUGE
In stockinette stitch on US 4 (3.5 mm) needles:
22 sts and 44 rows = 4 x 4 in (10 x 10 cm)

Instructions

In Pale Blush, CO 105 sts. The last 5 sts of these are the stk-sts.

Rnd 1: Selv st, p3, k2tog, yo, k1, p1, * p1, k1, yo, skp, p6, k2tog, yo, k1, p1 *, rep from * to * 5 times more, p1, k1, yo, skp, p3, selv st, k5 (stk-sts).

Rnd 2 and all other even-numbered rnds: Work all sts as they appear, knit the yo's.

Rnd 3: Selv st, p2, k2tog, yo, k2, p1, * p1, k2, yo, skp, p4, k2tog, yo, k2, p1 *, rep from * to * 5 times more, p1, k2, yo, skp, p2, selv st, k5 (stk-sts).

Rnd 5: Selv st, p1, k2tog, yo, k3, p1, * p1, k3, yo, skp, p2, k2tog, yo, k3, p1 *, rep from * to * 5 times more, p1, k3, yo, skp, p1, selv st, k5 (stk-sts).

Rnd 7: Selv st, p1, k3, k2tog, yo, p1, * p1, yo, skp, k3, p2, k3, k2tog, yo, p1 *, rep from * to * 5 times more, p1, yo, skp, k3, p1, selv st, k5 (stk-sts).

Rnd 9: Selv st, p1, k2, k2tog, yo, p2, * p2, yo, skp, k2, p2, k2, k2tog, yo, p2*, rep from * to * 5 times more, p2, yo, skp, k2, p1, selv st, k5 (stk-sts).

Rnd 11: Selv st, p1, k1, k2tog, yo, p3, * p3, yo, skp, k1, p2, k1, k2tog, yo, p3 *, rep from * to * 5 times more, p3, yo, skp, k1, p1, selv st, k5 (stk-sts).

Rnd 13: Selv st, p1, k2, p4, * p3, hold 4 sts on cable needle behind work, p1, k2, p1, then p1, k2, p1 from the cable needle, p3 *, rep from * to * 5 times more, p4, k2, p1, selv st, k5 (stk-sts).

Rnd 15: Selv st, p1, k1, yo, skp, p3, * p3, k2tog, yo, k1, p2, k1, yo, skp, p3 *, rep from

* to * 5 times more, p3, k2tog, yo, k1, p1, selv st, k5 (stk-sts).

Rnd 17: Selv st, p1, k2, yo, skp, p2, * p2, k2tog, yo, k2, p2, k2, yo, skp, p2 *, rep from * to * 5 times more, p2, k2tog, yo, k2, p1, selv st, k5 (stk-sts).

Rnd 19: Selv st, p1, k3, yo, skp, p1, * p1, k2tog, yo, k3, p2, k3, yo, skp, p1 *, rep from * to * 5 times more, p1, k2tog, yo, k3, p1, selv st, k5 (stk-sts).

Rnd 21: Selv st, p1, yo, skp, k3, p1, * p1, k3, k2tog, yo, p2, yo, skp, k3, p1 *, rep from * to * 5 times more, p1, k3, k2tog, yo, p1, selv st, k5 (stk-sts).

Rnd 23: Selv st, p2, yo, skp, k2, p1, * p1, k2, k2tog, yo, p4, yo, skp, k2, p1 *, rep from * to * 5 times more, p1, k2, k2tog, yo, p2, selv st, k5 (stk-sts).

Rnd 25: Selv st, p3, yo, skp, k1, p1, * p1, k1, k2tog, yo, p6, yo, skp, k1, p1 *, rep from * to * 5 times more, p1, k1, k2tog, yo, p3, selv st, k5 (stk-sts).

Rnd 27: Selv st, * p3, hold 4 sts on cable needle in front of work, p1, k2, p1, then p1, k2, p1 from the cable needle, p6, hold 4 sts on cable needle in front of work, p1, k2, p1, then p1, k2, p1 from the cable needle, p3 *, rep from * to * 2 times more, p3, hold 4 sts on cable needle in front of work, p1, k2, p1, then p1, k2, p1 from the cable needle, p3, selv st, k5 (stk-sts).

Repeat Rnds 1–28 another 14 times; then knit 2 rounds, and transfer the sts to a spare cord or piece of waste yarn for holding.

Now, secure the steek as described in Basics (pp. 16–17); then cut it.

Place the formerly held sts onto a circular needle with long cord. In White, knit 1 row, knitting every 3rd and 4th stitch together = 75 sts; then p/u and knit sts from the selvedge as follows: 1 additional st at the corner, 290 sts from the long edge, 1 st at the corner, 75 sts from the short edge, 1 st at the corner, an additional 290 sts from the other long edge, and 1 st at the corner. (734 sts)

Now, work 6 rounds in garter stitch; at the same time, in every other round, always before and after the corner stitch, M1-p (758 sts); transfer the sts to a spare cord or piece of waste yarn for holding. P/u the same number of sts from the back of the selvedge stitches, and here, too, work 6 rounds in garter stitch, at the same time working increases as previously described. In the next rnd, knit the sts from the RS and WS together in pairs, always 1 st from the RS with 1 st from the WS.

CONTINUE

Rnd 1: In White, knit.
Rnd 2: In Pale Blush, purl, while at the same time, always before and after the corner stitch, M1-p.
Repeat Rnds 1–2 as often as desired; then BO all sts, using elastic BO method (see p. 25).

FINISHING

Wash the stole according to the manufacturer's recommendations on the ball band of the yarn, pin it to block, and let it dry. Carefully weave in the remaining ends.

KNITTING CHART

Refer to key on p. 26.

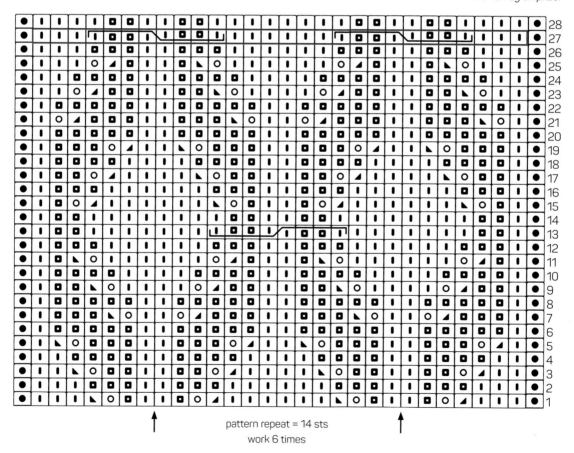

pattern repeat = 14 sts
work 6 times

Exception: In Rnd 27, the pattern repeat needs 28 sts, and is therefore worked only 3 times around (marked in red).

Saga
THREE-COLOR SHOULDER PLAID

Basics

FINISHED SIZE
43.3 x 27.6 in (110 x 70 cm)

TOOLS AND MATERIALS
▶ Rowan Alpaca Soft DK (70% wool, 30% alpaca; 136 yd/125 m, 1.75 oz/50 g per skein); 4 skeins #211 Charcoal, 3 skeins #207 Mulberry, and 2 skeins #208 Autumn Purple
▶ Circular knitting needles, US size 6 (4.0 mm) in different lengths
▶ Stitch markers as needed
▶ Scissors
▶ Tapestry needle for weaving in ends

STITCH PATTERNS
Main pattern for the body: Alternate k4, p2.
Slipped stitch: Slip the st with yarn in back of work.
Honeycomb pattern: See written instructions.
Steek stitches: Worked as knit sts and not counted in the stitch count.

GAUGE
In stockinette stitch on US 6 (4.0 mm) needles:
22 sts and 30 rows = 4 x 4 in (10 x 10 cm)

Instructions

CO 123 sts in Charcoal; immediately join into the round, taking care to not twist the sts of the CO row.
Rnd 1: K the selv st, * k4, p2 *, rep from * to * 18 times more, k4, k the selv st, k3 (stk-sts).
Work a total of 176 rnds as set; then BO all sts loosely.
Now, secure the steek as described in Basics (pp. 16–17); then cut it.
Then, in Autumn Purple, p/u and knit sts as follows: 130 sts from the selvedge sts of the long edges, 118 sts each along the short edges, and 1 st at every corner. (500 sts)

BEGIN BORDER
Work in the round, beginning at a long edge.
Rnd 1: K the corner stitch, M1-k, k130, M1-k, k the corner stitch, M1-k, k118, M1-k, k the corner stitch, M1-k, k130, M1-k, k the corner stitch, M1-k, k118, M1-k. (508 sts)
Rnd 2: K508.
Rnds 3–4: Work as Rnds 1–2 (516 sts).
Transfer all sts to a spare cord or piece of waste yarn for holding.
P/u the same number of sts in the same configuration on the WS of the shawl, always inserting the needle into the unused

leg of the stitch that you already picked up on the RS earlier, and work Rnds 1–4. Knit sts are visible on the outside. Now, knit the sts from the RS and WS together in pairs, always 1 st from the RS with 1 st from the WS.

HONEYCOMB PATTERN
Now, continue in Honeycomb pattern, as follows:
Rnd 1: In Autumn Purple, purl all sts; at the same time, before and after every corner stitch, M1-p, k the corner stitch. (524 sts)
Rnd 2: In Mulberry, k the corner stitch, k4, * slip 2 sts, k4 *, rep from * to * 21 times more, k the corner stitch, k4, * slip 2 sts, k4 *, rep from * to * 19 times more, k the corner stitch, k4, * slip 2 sts, k4 *, rep from * to * 21 times more, k the corner stitch, k4, * slip 2 sts, k4 *, rep from * to * 19 times more.
Rnd 3: In Mulberry, work as Rnd 2 but before and after every corner stitch, M1-k. (532 sts)
Rnd 4: In Autumn Purple, knit all sts.
Rnd 5: In Autumn Purple, purl all sts; at the same time, before and after every corner stitch, M1-p, k the corner stitch. (540 sts)

Rnds 6–21: Work Rnds 2–5 another 4 times. (604 sts)

From here on, continue in Mulberry only in main pattern for the body, dividing sts in sections as follows:

Rnd 22: K the corner stitch, * k4, p2 *, rep from * to * 25 times more, k the corner stitch, * p2, k4 *, rep from * to * 23 times more, k the corner stitch, * k4, p2 *, rep from * to * 25 times more, k the corner stitch, * p2, k4 *, rep from * to * 23 times more.

Rnd 23: K the corner stitch, M1-p, * k4, p2 *, rep from * to * 25 times more, M1-k, k the corner stitch, M1-k, * p2, k4 *, rep from * to * 23 times more, M1-p, k the corner stitch, M1-p, * k4, p2 *, rep from * to * 25 times more, M1-k, k the corner stitch, M1-k, * p2, k4 *, rep from * to * 23 times more, M1-p. (612 sts)

Rnds 24–35: Rep Rnds 22–23 another 6 times, while incorporating increased sts into the stitch patt. (660 sts)

BO all sts, using elastic BO method (see p. 25).

FINISHING

Wash the shoulder plaid according to the manufacturer's recommendations on the ball band of the yarn, pin it to block, and let it dry. Carefully weave in the remaining ends.

SEMICIRCULAR SHAWL WITH NUPPS

FINISHED SIZE
59 x 21.3 in (150 x 54 cm)

TOOLS AND MATERIALS
▶ Lang Yarns Cashmere Classic (100% cashmere; 55 yd/50 m, 0.9 oz/25 g per skein); 7 skeins #0029 Lobster and 5 skeins #0003 Gray
▶ Circular knitting needles, US size 10½ (7.0 mm) in different lengths
▶ DPN set, US size 10½ (7.0 mm)
▶ Crochet hook, US size H-8 (5.0 mm)
▶ Stitch markers as needed
▶ Scissors
▶ Tapestry needle for weaving in ends

STITCH PATTERNS
Main pattern in rounds: Rnds 1–2 in Gray: knit; Rnd 3 in Lobster: knit; Rnd 4 in Lobster: purl, carrying up the working yarn in the unused color loosely in back of work.
Border: Work 3 sts before (to the right of) and after (to the left of) the main patt in garter stitch, always alternating Rnd 1: knit and Rnd 2: purl.
Nupp (N): Insert the crochet hook into the indicated stitch, pull the working yarn through to form a loop, * place the working yarn around the hook, insert the crochet hook into the same stitch again, and pull the working yarn through *, rep from * to * 3 times more. Pull the working yarn

through all loops on the hook, place the working yarn around the hook again, and pull it through the single loop. Now, insert the hook from the back into the stitch below the nupp, grasp the working yarn, and pull it through both loops on the hook at once. Place the finished nupp onto the right needle.
Steek stitches: Worked as knit sts at a slightly tighter gauge than usual and not counted in the stitch count.

GAUGE
In stockinette stitch on US 7 (7.0 mm) needles:
16 sts and 22 rows = 4 x 4 in (10 x 10 cm)

Instructions

CO 5 sts in Gray.
Row 1: In Gray, k5.
Row 2: In Gray, k2, M1-k, k1, M1-k, k2. (7 sts)
Row 3: In Lobster, k3, M1-k, k1, M1-k, k3. (9 sts)
Row 4: In Lobster, k3, M1-k, k3, M1-k, k3. (11 sts)
Row 5: In Gray, k3, M1-k, k5, M1-k, k3. (13 sts)
Row 6: In Gray, k3, M1-p, p7, M1-p, k3. (15 sts)

Row 7: In Lobster, k3, M1-k, k9, M1-k, k3. (17 sts)
Row 8: In Lobster, k3, M1-k, k5, M1-k, place marker, k1 (ctr-st), place marker, M1-k, k5, M1-k, k3. (21 sts)
Now, CO an additional 5 sts for the steek, join into the round, and then distribute the sts onto a DPN set.
Rnds 1–4 show basic increases—a total of 10 increases in 4 rnds.
Please note the main pattern:
Rnd 1: In Gray, k3, M1-k, k15, M1-k, k3, k5 (stk-sts). (23 sts)
Rnd 2: In Gray, p3, M1-k, k17, M1-k, p3, k5 (stk-sts). (25 sts)
Rnd 3: In Lobster, k3, M1-k, k19, M1-k, k3, k5 (stk-sts). (27 sts)
Rnd 4: In Lobster, p3, M1-p, p10, M1-p, p1 (ctr-st), M1-p, p10, M1-p, p3, k5 (stk-sts). (31 sts)
Rnds 5–7: Work as Rnds 1–3. (37 sts)
Rnd 8: In Lobster, p3, M1-p, p4, 1 N, p4, 1 N, p5, M1-p, p1 (ctr-st), M1-p, p5, 1 N, p4, 1 N, p4, M1-p, p3, k5 (stk-sts). (41 sts)
Rnds 9–40: Work Rnds 5–8 another 8 times, always working 1 nupp more in every purled Rnd 8 in Lobster; after the last nupp before the center st: p4, 1 N, after the center st, work back mirror-inverted (reversing the order of sts) = for each one of the two halves, 10 nupps in the last rnd. (121 sts)
Rnds 41–43: Work as Rnds 1–3. (127 sts)

Rnd 44: In Lobster, p3, M1-p, p4, 1 N, p4, 1 N, p50, M1-p, p1 (ctr-st), M1-p, p50, 1 N, p4, 1 N, p4, M1-p, p3, k5 (stk-sts). (131 sts)

Rnds 45–76: Rep Rnds 41–44 another 8 times, always working 1 nupp more in every purled Rnd 44 in Lobster; after the last nupp before the center st: p4, 1 N, after the center st, work back mirror-inverted (reversing the order of sts) = for each one of the two halves, 10 nupps in the last rnd. (211 sts)

Rnds 77–79: Work as Rnds 1–3. (217 sts)

Rnd 80: In Lobster, p3, M1-p, p4, 1 N, p4, 1 N, p95, M1-p, p1 (ctr-st), M1-p, p95, 1 N, p4, 1 N, p4, M1-p, p3, k5 (stk-sts). (221 sts)

Rnds 81–92: Rep Rnds 77–80 another 3 times, always working 1 nupp more in every purled Rnd 80 in Lobster; after the last nupp before the center st: p4, 1 N, after the center st, work back mirror-inverted (reversing the order of sts) = for each one of the two halves, 5 nupps in the last rnd. (251 sts)

Rnds 93–94: In Gray, work as Rnds 1–2 (255 sts); then BO the 5 stk-sts. Knit 1 rnd more in Lobster. (257 sts) In the next row, BO all sts, using elastic BO method (see p. 25).

FINISHING

Secure the steek as described in Basics (pp. 16–17); then cut it. In Lobster, p/u and knit a sufficient number of sts from the cut edge, purl 1 WS row, and then knit 4 rows. BO all sts loosely, fold over to the WS, pin, and sew on. Treat the other cut edge the same way.

Alva

TRIANGULAR SHAWL IN KNIT-PURL PATTERN WITH PICOT EDGING

Basics

FINISHED SIZE
75 x 33.5 in (190 x 85 cm)

TOOLS AND MATERIALS
▶ Woll Butt Primo Ava (63% alpaca, 37% cotton; 246 yd/225 m, 1.75 oz/50 g per skein); 4 skeins #11571 Gray
▶ Circular knitting needles, US size 6 (4.0 mm) in different lengths
▶ DPN set, US size 6 (4.0 mm)
▶ Stitch markers as needed
▶ Scissors
▶ Tapestry needle for weaving in ends

STITCH PATTERNS
Garter stitch: In rows: knit all sts in all rows; in rounds, alternate—Rnd 1: knit; Rnd 2: purl.
Selvedge stitches: Work the first and the last 2 sts in garter stitch.
Ribbing: Alternate k1-tbl, p1.
Stockinette stitch: In rounds: knit all sts.
Steek stitches: Worked as knit sts and not counted in the stitch count.

GAUGE
In stockinette stitch on US 6 (4.0 mm) needles:
20 sts and 32 rows = 4 x 4 in (10 x 10 cm)

Instructions

CO 5 sts.
Row 1: K2, yo, k1, yo, k2. (7 sts)
Row 2: K2, k-tbl of yo, yo, p1, yo, k-tbl of yo, k2. (9 sts)
Row 3: K2, yo, k1, k-tbl of yo, yo, k1 (ctr st; if helpful, place a marker before and after the center st), yo, k-tbl of yo, k1, yo, k2. (13 sts)
Row 4: K2, k-tbl of yo, k2, k-tbl of yo, p1, k-tbl of yo, k2, k-tbl of yo, k2.
Row 5: K2, yo, k4, yo, k1, yo, k4, yo, k2. (17 sts)
Row 6: K2, k-tbl of yo, k4, k-tbl of yo, p1, k-tbl of yo, k4, k-tbl of yo, k2.
Row 7: K2, yo, k6, yo, k1, yo, k6, yo, k2. (21 sts)
Row 8: K2, k-tbl of yo, k6, k-tbl of yo, p1, k-tbl of yo, k6, k-tbl of yo, k2.
Row 9: K2, yo, k8, yo, k1, yo, k8, yo, k2. (25 sts)
After this row, CO an additional 9 sts for the steek, join work into the round, and distribute sts onto a DPN set.
Rnd 1: P2, p-tbl of yo, p8, p-tbl of yo, k1, p-tbl of yo, p8, p-tbl of yo, p2, k9 (stk-sts).
Rnd 2: K2, yo, k10, yo, k1, yo, k10, yo, k2, k9 (stk-sts). (29 sts)
Rnds 3–15: Rep Rnds 1–2 another 6 times; then work only Rnd 1 once more. (53 sts)

Rnd 16: K2, yo, k24, yo, k1, yo, k24, yo, k2, k9 (stk-sts). (57 sts)
Rnd 17: P2, k-tbl of yo, k24, k-tbl of yo, k1, k-tbl of yo, k24, k-tbl of yo, p2, k9 (stk-sts).
Rnds 18–29: Rep Rnds 16–17 another 6 times. (81 sts)
Rnd 30: K2, yo, k38, yo, k1, yo, k38, yo, k2, k9 (stk-sts). (85 sts)
Rnd 31: P2, p-tbl of yo, p38, p-tbl of yo, k1, p-tbl of yo, p38, p-tbl of yo, p2, k9 (stk-sts).
Rnds 32–33: Work as Rnds 30–31. (89 sts)
Rnds 34–105: Rep Rnds 16–33 another 4 times. (233 sts)
Rnd 106: K2, yo, * ssk, yo *, rep from * to * 55 times more, k2, yo, k1, yo, k2, * yo, skp *, rep from * to * 55 times more, yo, k2, k9 (stk-sts). (237 sts)
Rnd 107: P2, p-tbl of yo, * k1-tbl, p1 *, rep from * to * 56 times more, k-tbl of yo, k1, k-tbl of yo, * p1, k1-tbl *, rep from * to * 56 times more, p-tbl of yo, p2, k9 (stk-sts).
Rnds 108–123: Rep Rnds 106–107 another 8 times. (269 sts)
Rnd 124: K2, yo, p1, * k1-tbl, p5, k1-tbl, p3, k1-tbl, p1, k1-tbl, p7 *, rep from * to * 5 times more, k1-tbl, p5, k1-tbl, p3, k1-tbl, yo, k1, yo, k1-tbl, p3, k1-tbl, p5, k1-tbl, * p7, k1-tbl, p1, k1-tbl, p3, k1-tbl, p5, k1-tbl *, rep from * to * 5 times more, p1, yo, k2, k9 (stk-sts). (273 sts)

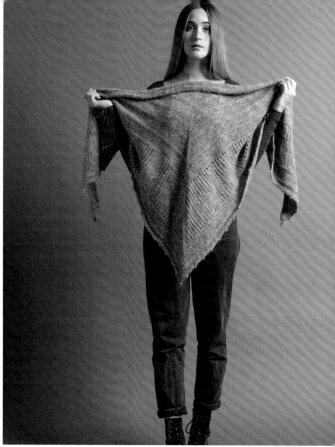

Rnd 125: P2, p-tbl of yo, p1, * k1-tbl, p5, k1-tbl, p3, k1-tbl, p1, k1-tbl, p7 *, rep from * to * 5 times more, k1-tbl, p5, k1-tbl, p3, k1-tbl, p-tbl of yo, k1, p-tbl of yo, k1-tbl, p3, k1-tbl, p5, k1-tbl, * p7, k1-tbl, p1, k1-tbl, p3, k1-tbl, p5, k1-tbl *, rep from * to * 5 times more, p1, p-tbl of yo, p2, k9 (stk-sts).

Rnds 126–135: Rep Rnds 124–125 another 5 times, always either k-tbl or p-tbl of yo's according to the pattern. (293 sts)

Rnd 136: K2, yo, * p1, k1-tbl *, rep from * to * 71 times more, yo, k1, yo, * k1-tbl, p1 *, rep from * to * 71 times more, yo, k2, k9 (stk-sts). (297 sts)

Rnd 137: P2, k-tbl of yo, * p1, k1-tbl *, rep from * to * 71 times more, p-tbl of yo, k1, p-tbl of yo, * k1-tbl, p1 *, rep from * to * 71 times more, k-tbl of yo, p2, k9 (stk-sts).

Rnds 138–145: Rep Rnds 136–137 another 4 times, always either k-tbl or p-tbl of yo's, according to the pattern. (313 sts)

Rnd 146: K2, yo, * skp, yo *, rep from * to * 76 times more, k1, * yo, k2tog *, rep from * to * 76 times more, yo, k2, k9 (stk-sts). (315 sts)

Rnd 147: P2, p-tbl of yo, p154, k1, p154, p-tbl of yo, p2, k9 (stk-sts).

Rnd 148: K2, yo, k155, yo, k1, yo, k155, yo, k2, k9 (stk-sts). (319 sts)

Rnd 149: P2, p-tbl of yo, p155, p-tbl of yo, k1, p-tbl of yo, p155, p-tbl of yo, p2, k9 (stk-sts).

Rnd 150: K2, yo, k157, yo, k1, yo, k157, yo, k2, k9 (stk-sts). (323 sts)

Rnd 151: P2, k-tbl of yo, k157, k-tbl of yo, k1, k-tbl of yo, k157, k-tbl of yo, p2, k9 (stk-sts).

Rnds 152–163: Rep Rnds 150–151 another 6 times. (347 sts)

Rnd 164: K2, yo, k171, yo, k1, yo, k171, yo, k2, k9 (stk-sts). (351 sts)

Rnd 165: P2, p-tbl of yo, p171, p-tbl of yo, k1, p-tbl of yo, p171, p-tbl of yo, p2, k9 (stk-sts).

Rnds 166–167: Rep Rnds 164–165 once more. (355 sts)

Afterward, BO the 9 stk-sts knitwise, and BO all other sts with Picot edging as follows: Make 3 sts from the first st, BO 7 sts, * make 2 sts from the next st, BO 7 sts *, rep from * to * until all sts have been used up.

FINISHING

Now, secure the steek as described in Basics (pp. 16–17); then cut it. Fold over the stk-sts to the WS twice, pin, and sew on. Wash the shawl according to the manufacturer's recommendations on the ball band of the yarn, pin it to block, and let it dry. Carefully weave in the remaining ends.

TRIANGULAR SHAWL IN A PATTERN MIX

Basics

FINISHED SIZE
75.6 x 28.3 in (192 x 72 cm)

TOOLS AND MATERIALS
▶ Lang Yarns Carpe Diem (70% wool, 30% alpaca; 98 yd/90 m, 1.75 oz/50 g per skein); 9 skeins #0150 Mustard Yellow
▶ Circular knitting needles, US size 9 (5.5 mm) in different lengths
▶ DPN set, US size 9 (5.5 mm)
▶ Stitch markers as needed
▶ Scissors
▶ Tapestry needle for weaving in ends

STITCH PATTERNS
Stitch Pattern 1: Seed stitch
Row/Rnd 1: * K1, p1 *, rep from * to * to end.
Row/Rnd 2: * P1, k1 *, rep from * to * to end.
Please note: *Increasing 1 st each at the edge automatically shifts the stitch pattern in the round, which means "k1, p1" can be worked in every rnd.*
Stitch Pattern 2: Vertical stripes
* K4, p1 *, rep from * to * to end.
Stitch Pattern 3: Twisted rib
* P1, k1-tbl *, rep from * to * to end.
Stitch Pattern 4: Mini cables
Rnd 1: * Sl1, k1, yo, k1, pass the slipped st over the 2 knitted ones and the yo, p2 *, rep from * to * to end.

Rnds 2–4: * K3, p2 *, rep from * to * to end. Rep these 4 rnds all the time.
Stitch Pattern 5: Eyelet pattern
Rnd 1: * Yo, skp, k2 *, rep from * to * to end.
Rnd 2: Knit all sts.
Rnd 3: * K2, yo, skp *, rep from * to * to end.
Rnd 4: Knit all sts.
Selvedge stitches: In rows: as described for the row; in rounds: knit all selv sts in all rnds.
Steek stitches: Worked as knit sts and not counted in the stitch count.

GAUGE
In stockinette stitch on US 9 (5.5 mm) needles:
16 sts and 22 rows = 4 x 4 in (10 x 10 cm)

Tips
Increases are always worked by making a yarn over before/after the selvedge stitch, which is in the following row/round either knitted or purled through the back loop, depending on the pattern.
For ease of work, sections in different stitch patterns can be separated by stitch markers if needed.

Instructions

CO 3 sts.
Row 1: K1, yo, k1, yo, k1. (5 sts)
Row 2: P1, p-tbl of yo, k1, p-tbl of yo, p1.
Row 3: K1, yo, p1, k1, p1, yo, k1. (7 sts)
Row 4: P1, k-tbl of yo, p1, k1, p1, k-tbl of yo, p1.
Row 5: K1, yo, * k1, p1 *, rep from * to * once more, k1, yo, k1. (9 sts)
Row 6: P1, p-tbl of yo, * k1, p1 *, rep from * to * once more, k1, p-tbl of yo, p1.
Row 7: K1, yo, * p1, k1 *, rep from * to * 2 times more, p1, yo, k1. (11 sts)
Now, CO an additional 9 sts for the steek, join into the round, and distribute sts onto a DPN set.
Rnd 8: Selv st, yo, p-tbl of yo, * k1, p1 *, rep from * to * 2 times more, k1, p-tbl of yo, yo, selv st, k9 (stk-sts). (13 sts)
Rnd 9: Selv st, yo, p-tbl of yo, * k1, p1 *, rep from * to * 3 times more, k1, p-tbl of yo, yo, selv st, k9 (stk-sts). (15 sts)
Rnds 10–23: Work 14 rnds more in Stitch Pattern 1 as described for Rnds 8–9, incorporating the increased sts into the stitch patt (43 sts). When enough sts have accumulated, change to a circular needle with short cord.
Rnd 24: Selv st, yo, p-tbl of yo, 38 sts in Stitch Pattern 1, k1, k-tbl of yo (begin Stitch Pattern 2), yo, selv st, k9 (stk-sts). (45 sts)

Rnd 25: Selv st, yo, p-tbl of yo, 39 sts in Stitch Pattern 1, k2, k-tbl of yo, yo, selv st, k9 (stk-sts). (47 sts)

Rnd 26: Selv st, yo, p-tbl of yo, 40 sts in Stitch Pattern 1, k3, k-tbl of yo, yo, selv st, k9 (stk-sts). (49 sts)

Rnd 27: Selv st, yo, p-tbl of yo, 41 sts in Stitch Pattern 1, k4, p-tbl of yo, yo, selv st, k9 (stk-sts). (51 sts)

Rnd 28: Selv st, yo, p-tbl of yo, 42 sts in Stitch Pattern 1, k4, p1, k-tbl of yo, yo, selv st, k9 (stk-sts). (53 sts)

Rnd 29: Selv st, yo, p-tbl of yo, 43 sts in Stitch Pattern 1, k4, p1, k1, k-tbl of yo, yo, selv st, k9 (stk-sts). (55 sts)

Rnd 30: Selv st, yo, p-tbl of yo, 44 sts in Stitch Pattern 1, k4, p1, k2, k-tbl of yo, yo, selv st, k9 (stk-sts). (57 sts)

Rnd 31: Selv st, yo, p-tbl of yo, 45 sts in Stitch Pattern 1, k4, p1, k3, k-tbl of yo, yo, selv st, k9 (stk-sts). (59 sts)

Rnd 32: Selv st, yo, p-tbl of yo, 46 sts in Stitch Pattern 1, k4, p1, k4, p-tbl of yo, yo, selv st, k9 (stk-sts). (61 sts)

Rnd 33: Selv st, yo, p-tbl of yo, 47 sts in Stitch Pattern 1, 10 sts in Stitch Pattern 2, k-tbl of yo, yo, selv st, k9 (stk-sts). (63 sts)

Rnds 34–44: Work 11 rnds more in established patt, incorporating sts increased at the beginning of the rnd into Stitch Pattern 1 and sts increased at the end of the rnd into Stitch Pattern 2 (85 sts). In the next rnd, Stitch Pattern 3 will be additionally introduced.

Rnd 45: Selv st, yo, k-tbl of yo, * p1, k1-tbl *, rep from * to * 9 times more, p1 (= 21 sts in Stitch Pattern 3), place marker, 38 sts in Stitch Pattern 1, 22 sts in Stitch Pattern 2, k-tbl of yo, yo, selv st, k9 (stk-sts). (87 sts)

Rnd 46: Selv st, yo, p-tbl of yo, * k1-tbl, p1 *, rep from * to * 10 times more (= 22 sts in Stitch Pattern 3), slip marker, 38 sts in Stitch Pattern 1, 23 sts in Stitch Pattern 2, k-tbl of yo, yo, selv st, k9 (stk-sts). (89 sts)

Rnd 47: Selv st, yo, k-tbl of yo, * p1, k1-tbl *, rep from * to * 10 times more, p1 (= 23 sts in Stitch Pattern 3), slip marker, 38 sts in Stitch Pattern 1, 24 sts in Stitch Pattern 2, k-tbl of yo, yo, selv st, k9 (stk-sts). (91 sts)

Rnd 48: Selv st, yo, p-tbl of yo, * k1-tbl, p1 *, rep from * to * 11 times more (= 24 sts in Stitch Pattern 3), slip marker, 38 sts in Stitch Pattern 1, 25 sts in Stitch Pattern 2, k-tbl of yo, yo, selv st, k9 (stk-sts). (93 sts)

Rnds 49–69: Rep Rnd 48 an additional 21 times, incorporating sts increased at the beginning of the rnd into Stitch Pattern 3 and sts increased at the end of the rnd into Stitch Pattern 2. (135 sts)

Rnd 70: Selv st, yo, k-tbl of yo, 46 sts in Stitch Pattern 3, slip marker, 38 sts in Stitch Pattern 1, 47 sts in Stitch Pattern 2, k-tbl of yo, yo, selv st, k9 (stk-sts). (137 sts)

In the next rnd, an additional block in Stitch Pattern 1 will be worked (remove markers as needed).

Rnd 71: Selv st, yo, k-tbl of yo, 18 sts in Stitch Pattern 1, 29 sts in Stitch Pattern 3, 38 sts in Stitch Pattern 1, 48 sts in Stitch Pattern 2, k-tbl of yo, yo, selv st, k9 (stk-sts). (139 sts)

Rnds 72–84: Rep Rnd 71 an additional 13 times, incorporating sts increased at the beginning of the rnd into Stitch Pattern 1 and sts increased at the end of the rnd

into Stitch Pattern 2. (165 sts)

In the next rnd, Stitch Patterns 4 and 5 will be additionally introduced.

Rnd 85: Selv st, yo, k-tbl of yo, 21 sts in stockinette stitch (= Stitch Pattern 5), 11 sts in Stitch Pattern 1, 29 sts in Stitch Pattern 3, 38 sts in Stitch Pattern 1, 40 sts in Stitch Pattern 2, p1, sl1, k1, yo, k1, pass the slipped st over the 2 knitted ones and the yo, * p2, sl1, k1, yo, k1, pass the slipped st over the 2 knitted ones and the yo *, rep from * to * 2 times more, p2, k1 (= 22 sts in Stitch Pattern 4), k-tbl of yo, yo, selv st, k9 (stk-sts). (167 sts)

Rnd 86: Selv st, yo, k-tbl of yo, k22 (= Stitch Pattern 5), 11 sts in Stitch Pattern 1, 29 sts in Stitch Pattern 3, 38 sts in Stitch Pattern 1, 40 sts in Stitch Pattern 2, p1, k3, * p2, k3 *, rep from * to * 2 times more, p2, k2 (= 23 sts in Stitch Pattern 4), k-tbl of yo, yo, selv st, k9 (stk-sts). (169 sts)

Rnd 87: Selv st, yo, k-tbl of yo, k3, * yo, skp, k2 *, rep from * to * 4 times more (= 23 sts in Stitch Pattern 5), 11 sts in Stitch Pattern 1, 29 sts in Stitch Pattern 3, 38 sts in Stitch Pattern 1, 40 sts in Stitch Pattern 2, 24 sts in Stitch Pattern 4, k-tbl of yo, yo, selv st, k9 (stk-sts). (171 sts)

Rnd 88: Selv st, yo, k-tbl of yo, 24 sts in Stitch Pattern 5, 11 sts in Stitch Pattern 1, 29 sts in Stitch Pattern 3, 38 sts in Stitch Pattern 1, 40 sts in Stitch Pattern 2, 25 sts in Stitch Pattern 4, k-tbl of yo, yo, selv st, k9 (stk-sts). (173 sts)

Rnd 89: Selv st, yo, k-tbl of yo, k1, * k2, yo, skp *, rep from * to * 5 times more (= 25 sts in Stitch Pattern 5), 11 sts in Stitch Pattern 1, 29 sts in Stitch Pattern 3, 38 sts in Stitch Pattern 1, 40 sts in Stitch

Pattern 2, 26 sts in Stitch Pattern 4, k-tbl of yo, yo, selv st, k9 (stk-sts). (175 sts)

Rnds 90–119: As established in Rnd 89, work 30 rnds more, incorporating sts increased at the beginning of the rnd into Stitch Pattern 5 and sts increased at the end of the rnd into Stitch Pattern 4. (235 sts)

Rnd 120: Selv st, yo, k-tbl of yo, 16 sts in Stitch Pattern 1, 40 sts in Stitch Pattern 5, 11 sts in Stitch Pattern 1, 29 sts in Stitch Pattern 3, 38 sts in Stitch Pattern 1, 40 sts in Stitch Pattern 2, 57 sts in Stitch Pattern 4, k-tbl of yo, yo, selv st, k9 (stk-sts). (237 sts)

Rnds 121–155: As established in Rnd 120, work the final 35 rnds of the shawl, incorporating sts increased at the beginning of the rnd into Stitch Pattern 1 and sts increased at the end of the rnd into Stitch Pattern 4. (307 sts)

Rnd 156: Selv st, yo, k-tbl of yo, * p1, k1 *, rep from * to * to the last st, k1, p-tbl of yo, yo, selv st, BO the 9 stk-sts knitwise, and continue in back-and-forth rows with turning. (309 sts)

Rows 157–159: As established in Rnd 156, work 3 rows more (remembering to maintain pattern on WS row); then BO all sts in pattern.

FINISHING

Secure the steek as described in Basics (pp. 16–17); then cut it. Fold the steek sts over to the WS two times, pin in place, and sew on.

Wash the shawl according to the manufacturer's recommendations on the ball band of the yarn, pin it to block, and let it dry. Carefully weave in the remaining ends.

BROAD STOLE IN A LACE PATTERN

Basics

FINISHED SIZE
71 x 20.5 in (180 x 52 cm)

TOOLS AND MATERIALS
▶ Rosy Green Wool Cheeky Merino Joy (100% wool; 350 yd/320 m, 3.5 oz/100 g per skein); 5 skeins #053 Sand
▶ Circular knitting needle, US size 9 (5.5 mm), 32 in (80 cm) long
▶ Stitch markers as needed
▶ Scissors
▶ Tapestry needle for weaving in ends

FINISHED SIZE
71 x 20.5 in (180 x 52 cm)

PATTERN NOTE
The stole is worked with yarn held double.

STITCH PATTERNS
Selvedge stitches: In rows: slip the first st, knit the last st; in rounds: knit all selv sts in all rounds.

Garter stitch: In rows: knit all sts in all rows; in rounds, alternate—Rnd 1: knit; Rnd 2: purl.

Lace pattern: See written instructions and chart. In the chart, all rounds are shown. Read the chart from right to left.

Steek stitches: Worked as knit sts and not counted in the stitch count.

Tip
Since the stole is worked with yarn held double, it is recommended that you wind one of the skeins into 2 balls of 1.75 oz (50 g) each prior to starting.

GAUGE
With two strands of yarn held together in stockinette stitch on US 9 (5.5 mm) needles:
20 sts and 22 rows = 4 x 4 in (10 x 10 cm)

Instructions

With yarn held double, CO 86 sts and work 6 rows in garter stitch.

In the last row, CO 9 additional sts for the steek and join into the round.

Rnd 1: Selv st, k84, selv st, k9 (stk-sts).

Rnd 2: Selv st, p84, selv st, k9 (stk-sts).

Rnd 3: Selv st, k4, * k9, yo, skp, k8 *, rep from * to * 3 times more, k4, selv st, k9 (stk-sts).

Rnd 4: Selv st, p3, k1, * k5, p3, k1, k the yo, k1, p3, k5 *, rep from * to * 3 times more, k1, p3, selv st, k9 (stk-sts).

Rnd 5: Selv st, k4, * k7, k2tog, yo, k1, yo, skp, k7 *, rep from * to * 3 times more, k4, selv st, k9 (stk-sts).

Rnd 6: Selv st, p4, * p7, k5, p7 *, rep from * to * 3 times more, p4, selv st, k9 (stk-sts).

Rnd 7: Selv st, k4, * k6, k2tog, yo, k3, yo, skp, k6 *, rep from * to * 3 times more, k4, selv st, k9 (stk-sts).

Rnd 8: Selv st, p3, k1, * k3, p3, k7, p3, k3 *, rep from * to * 3 times more, k1, p3, selv st, k9 (stk-sts).

Rnd 9: Selv st, k4, * k5, k2tog, yo, k5, yo, skp, k5 *, rep from * to * 3 times more, k4, selv st, k9 (stk-sts).

Rnd 10: Selv st, p4, * p5, k9, p5 *, rep from * to * 3 times more, p4, selv st, k9 (stk-sts).

Rnd 11: Selv st, k4, * k4, k2tog, yo, k7, yo, skp, k4 *, rep from * to * 3 times more, k4, selv st, k9 (stk-sts).

Rnd 12: Selv st, p3, k1, * k1, p3, k11, p3, k1 *, rep from * to * 3 times more, k1, p3, selv st, k9 (stk-sts).

Rnd 13: Selv st, k4, * k5, yo, skp, k5, k2tog, yo, k5 *, rep from * to * 3 times more, k4, selv st, k9 (stk-sts).

Rnd 14: Selv st, p4, * p4, k11, p4 *, rep from * to * 3 times more, p4, selv st, k9 (stk-sts).

Rnd 15: Selv st, k4, * k6, yo, skp, k3, k2tog, yo, k6 *, rep from * to * 3 times more, k4, selv st, k9 (stk-sts).

Rnd 16: Selv st, p3, k1, * k2, p3, k9, p3, k2 *, rep from * to * 3 times more, k1, p3, selv st, k9 (stk-sts).

Rnd 17: Selv st, k4, * k7, yo, skp, k1, k2tog, yo, k7 *, rep from * to * 3 times more, k4, selv st, k9 (stk-sts).

Rnd 18: Selv st, p4, * p6, k7, p6 *, rep from * to * 3 times more, p4, selv st, k9 (stk-sts).

Rnd 19: Selv st, k4, * k8, yo, sk2p, yo, k8 *, rep from * to * 3 times more, k4, selv st, k9 (stk-sts).

Rnd 20: Selv st, p3, k1, * k4, p3, k5, p3, k4 *, rep from * to * 3 times more, k1, p3, selv st, k9 (stk-sts).

Rep these 20 rnds 18 times more. In the last rnd, BO the 9 stk-sts; then work 6 rows more in garter stitch. Then BO all sts loosely.

FINISHING

Secure the steek as described in Basics (pp. 16–17); then cut it. Fold over the stk-sts to the WS twice, pin, and sew on. Wash the stole according to the manufacturer's recommendations on the ball band of the yarn, pin it to block, and let it dry. Carefully weave in the remaining ends.

KNITTING CHART

Refer to key on p. 26.

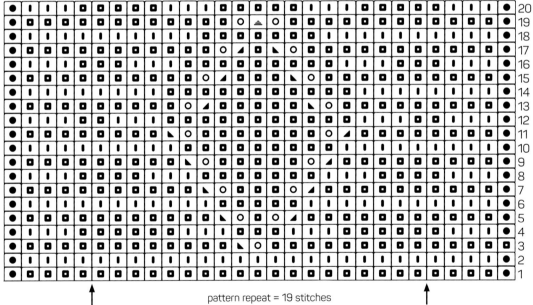

pattern repeat = 19 stitches
work 4 times

♡ ABOUT THE AUTHOR

At a tender preschool age, Andrea Brauneis made her first spool knit rugs for her dollhouse, and crafting pursuits have continued to captivate her ever since. More than 25 years ago, she had the great fortune to be able to turn her hobby into an occupation, thanks to professional design training and workshops, which have enabled her to constantly broaden her knowledge. Since then, she has worked as a designer and sample knitter for various yarn labels and a private customer base. She lives with her family in the out-skirts of Munich, Germany.

Watch: www.instagram/strickzeit
Knit with us: www.facebook.com/strickzeit/ZeitzumStricken

♡ ACKNOWLEDGMENTS

Just one year ago, I couldn't have imagined in my wildest dreams that I would become the author of a knitting book one day. From the first idea to the implementation and publishing of this book, I have had an incredible journey. The previous weeks and months have been filled with tension, suspension, joy, anticipation, numerous positive experiences, and plenty of work.

Here and now, it is time to say THANKS to all those who have made it possible for me to write this wonderful book.

First and foremost, I would like to thank my family, who fill me with joy, have always had my back, and have lived through the occasional stressful hour with me.

I would also like to say thanks to the wonderful team at EMF-Verlag publishers, who have made it possible to let this book become reality in the first place, especially my wonderful project manager, Anja Sommerfeld. Thank you, dear Ms. Sommerfeld, for implementing this beautiful project with me and for always having been available for me and my questions with never-ending patience.

To my editor, Ute Wielandt, too, I would like to say thank you for your exceptional work. You have checked all my texts and instructions in great detail, eliminated mistakes, and given the book as a whole a coherent structure.

My sample knitters and test knitters deserve much praise and a big thank-you too: Lila (Instagram.com/liladoesknit), Sylvia (Instagram.com/sylhell), Sonja (Instagram.com/sonjasstrickshop), Nina (Instagram.com/joni_madewithlove), Sandra (Instagram.com/frausonnenburg), Christine, Ilka, Lilly, Nora, and Luise.

With never-ending zeal, these great ladies have tirelessly knit, often until late into the night, checked the pattern instructions, sampled various yarns, and shown great trust in me, since all the designs were new to all of them.

And last but not least, thank you many, many times, dear sponsors: Lang Yarns, Buttinette, Rosy Green Wool, Rowan, Amano Yarns, Ito Yarn, and Prym, for your generous support with your wonderful yarns and knitting tools.